Timeless Books of Truth

When you're seeking a book on practical spiritual living, you want to know That It Is based on an authentic tradition of timeless teachings and that it resonates with integrity.

This is the goal of Crystal Clarity Publishers: to offer you books of practical wisdom filled with true spiritual principles that have not only been tested through the ages but also through personal experience.

Started in 1968, Crystal Clarity is the publishing house of Ananda, a spiritual community dedicated to meditation and living by true values, as shared by Paramhansa Yogananda and his direct disciple Swami Kriyananda, the founder of Ananda. The members of our staff and all of our authors live by these principles. Our work touches thousands around the world whose lives have been enriched by these universal teachings.

We publish only books that combine creative thinking, universal principles, and a timeless message. Crystal Clarity books will open doors to help you discover more fulfillment and joy by living and acting from the center of peace within you.

How to Love
and Be Loved

Paramhansa Yogananda

How to Love and Be Loved

Paramhansa Yogananda

Crystal Clarity Publishers
Nevada City, California

ISBN: 978-1-56589-316-0
eISBN: 978-1-56589-572-0
Printed in China
Designed by Crystal Clarity Publishers

Crystal Clarity Publishers
14618 Tyler Foote Road
Nevada City, CA 95959
800.424.1055 or 530.478.7600
clarity@crystalclarity.com
www.crystalclarity.com

Library of Congress Cataloging-in-Publication Data

Yogananda, Paramhansa, 1893-1952.
  Spiritual relationships / by Paramhansa Yogananda.
      p. cm.
  Includes index.
  ISBN 978-1-56589-224-8 (tradepaper, photos, index)
  1. Spirituality. 2. Self-Realization Fellowship. 3. Bible—Meditations.
4. Bhagavad gita—Meditations. I. Title. II. Series.

  BP605.S4Y6145 2007
  294.5'44--dc22

                        2007021414

Contents

Publisher's Note 9

1   Friendship 13

2   The Folly of Selfishness 29

3   How to Be a Friend 43

4   Spiritual Marriage & Family Life 61

     • *Creating a Spiritual Marriage* 63

     • *Sex: Right Use of the Creative Force* 88

     • *Parents and Children* 99

5   Separation and Loss 111

6   The Friend of All Friends 123

Index 139

List of Illustrations 149

About the Author 151

Further Explorations 153

Dear Reader:

What a wonderful vision of life Paramhansa Yogananda describes in these pages, as he examines all relationships and their divine potential. Always realistic, practical, and entertaining, Yogananda is not afraid to express the all-too-obvious challenges we face, and also to share clear and powerful solutions and directions.

Paramhansa Yogananda came to the United States from India in 1920, bringing to the West the teachings and techniques of yoga, the ancient science of soul awakening. He was the first master of yoga to make his home in the West, and his *Autobiography of a Yogi* has become the best-selling autobiography of all time, awakening fascination in Westerners with the spiritual teachings of the East.

Yoga is the ancient science of redirecting one's energies inward to produce spiritual awakening. In addition to bringing Americans the most practical and effective techniques of meditation, Yogananda showed how these principles can be applied to all areas of life. He was a prolific writer, lecturer, and composer. He lived in America 32 years, until his death in 1952.

The articles included in this book are taken from several sources: the lessons he wrote in the 1920s and 1930s;

articles of his that appeared in *Inner Culture* and *East West* magazines, published before 1943; the 1949 edition of *Whispers from Eternity*; and notes taken by Swami Kriyananda during the years he lived with Yogananda as a close disciple.

Our goal in this book is to let the Master's spirit come clearly through, with a minimum of editing. Sometimes sentences, redundant in the present context, have been deleted. Sometimes words or punctuation have been changed to clarify the meaning. Most of what is included here is not available elsewhere.

May Yogananda's words on spiritual relationships infuse your life with greater clarity, inspiration, and divine love.

Crystal Clarity Publishers

How to Love and Be Loved

THE ART OF GAINING FRIENDS

Friendship is God's love shining through the eyes of your loved ones, calling you home to drink His nectar of all selfishness-dissolving unity. Friendship is God's trumpet call, bidding the soul to destroy the partitions that separate it from other souls and from Him. True friendship unites two souls so completely that they reflect the unity of Spirit.

True friendship is broad and inclusive. Selfish attachment to a single individual, excluding all others, inhibits the development of divine friendship. Extend the boundaries of the glowing kingdom of your love, gradually including within them your family, your neighbors, your community, your country, all countries—in short, all sentient creatures. Be a cosmic friend, imbued with kindness and affection for all of God's creation, scattering love everywhere.

To have friends, you must manifest friendliness. If you open the door to the magnetic power of friendship, a soul or souls of like vibrations will be attracted to you. The more friendly you become toward *all*, the greater will be the number of your real friends.

When true friendship exists between two souls and they seek spiritual love and God's love together, when their only wish is to be of service to each other, their friendship produces the flame of Spirit. Through perfected divine friendship, mutually seeking spiritual perfection, you will find the one Great Friend.

Unfailing Laws of Friendship

Be neither unduly familiar with, nor indifferent to, a friend. Do not limit him by telling him, "I know all about you." Respect and love grow among friends with time. "Familiarity breeds contempt" between those who are mutually useless, selfish, material-minded, and unproductive of inspiration or self-development. The greater the mutual service, the deeper the friendship. Why does Jesus have such a wide following? Because He, like the other great masters, is unequaled in His service to humanity.

To attract friends you must possess the qualities of a real friend. Blind friendship may end in sudden, blind hate. The building of wisdom and spiritual understanding by mutual effort can bind two souls by the laws of everlasting divine love.

Human love and friendship have their basis in service on the physical, mental, or business plane. They are short-lived and conditional. Divine love has its foundation in service on the spiritual and intuitional planes, and is unconditional and eternal.

When perfect friendship exists, either between two hearts or within a group of hearts in a spiritual organization, such friendship perfects each individual. In the heart purified by friendship, one beholds an open door of unity through which one should invite other souls to enter—those who love him as well as those who love him not. When divine friendship reigns supreme in the temple of your heart, your soul will merge with the vast Cosmic Soul, leaving far behind the confining bonds which separated it from all of God's creation.

Consider no one a stranger. Learn to feel that everybody is your kin. Family love is merely one of the first exercises in the Divine Teacher's course in Friendliness, intended to prepare your heart for an all-inclusive love. Feel that the life-blood of God is circulating in the veins of all races. How does anyone dare to hate any human being of any race when he knows that God lives and breathes in all? We are Americans or Hindus or other nationalities for just a few years, but we are God's children forever. The soul cannot be confined within man-made boundaries: its nationality is Spirit, its country is Omnipresence.

This does not mean that you must know and love all human beings and creatures personally and individually. All you need to do is to be ready at all times to spread the light

of friendly service over all living creatures which you happen
to contact. This requires constant mental effort and prepared-
ness—in other words, unselfishness. The sun shines equally
on diamond and charcoal, but one has developed qualities
that enable it to reflect the sunlight brilliantly, while the other
absorbs all the sunlight. Emulate the diamond in your dealings
with people. Brightly reflect the light of God's love.

Why Love Your Enemies?

The secret of Christ's strength lay in his love for all,
even his enemies. Far better to conquer by love the heart
of a person who hates you than to vanquish such a one by
other means. To the ordinary man such a doctrine seems
absurd. He wants to return ten slaps for the one he has
received and add twice as many kicks for good measure.
Why should you love your enemy? Love him that you may
bring the healing rays of your love into his hatred-stricken
heart and burn away the partitions of misery that separate
your soul from another.

Avoid doing anything that brings harm to yourself or
to another. If you are self-indulgent, or if you encourage a
friend in his vices, you are an enemy disguised as a friend.
By being true to yourself and a true friend to others, you

gain the friendship of God. Your love will expand until it becomes the one Love which flows through all hearts.

The Heart of Friendship

I will remain in hearts as the unknown friend, ever rousing them to flaming feelings, silently urging them through their own noble thoughts to forsake their slumber of earthliness.

I will behold the person who now considers himself as my enemy to be in truth my divine brother hiding behind a veil of misunderstanding. I will tear aside this veil with the dagger of love so that, seeing my humble, forgiving understanding, he will receive the offering of my good will.

The door of my friendliness will ever be open equally for those brothers who hate me and for those who love me.

I will feel for others as I feel for myself. I will work out my salvation by serving my fellowman.

THE SOCIAL WAY TO OMNIPRESENCE

The social way to attain cosmic consciousness is to expand the germ of divine love within the soul. Too much love of your own ego confines the soul to the boundaries of the flesh. The soul is an omnipresent reflection of the all-pervading Spirit. The ego is the body-bound consciousness of the soul. The soul as ego forgets its omnipresence and considers itself limited by the body.

When the ego begins, through practical sympathy, to feel itself in other bodies, it begins to regain its forgotten omnipresence. Unlike the shortsighted worldly man, the divine soul works not only for himself as one body, but also for himself in the body of others. You must learn to seek nourishment, prosperity, healing, or wisdom, not for yourself in one body only, but for yourself in all bodies.

The social way of developing cosmic consciousness is to love your family, neighbors, country, and the whole world as yourself. You are the king, and the kingdom of your love includes not only all human beings, but also animals, flowers, stars, and all living creatures. Love all men as your brothers, love all women as your sisters, love all elderly men and women as your parents, and love all human beings—the black, brown, yellow, white, red, and olive-colored races—as your friends and brothers. This is the social way of attaining cosmic consciousness.

Wisdom in Friendship

Some souls at sight become our own;

Others, whom oft we meet, forever remain unknown.

And yet, in whispers Dame Wisdom says:

"To love your own and the unknown alike are Heaven's ways."

What Is True Friendship?

Friendship is the universal spiritual attraction that unites souls in the bond of divine love. If you open the door to the magnetic power of friendship, a soul or souls of like vibrations will be attracted to you. Friendship is a manifestation of God's love for you, expressed through your friends, who constitute the most valuable possessions a human being can have.

You attract those who are like you. That is the law of vibration. Friendship is eternal. If you can form a friendship through which God is awakened in you, that is the greatest of all friendships.

True friendship lies in seeking soul progress together. Friendship must never have a material end in view, or an object to be gained. Friendship is an ever-increasing consciousness of equality and the blending of souls without any physical objective.

Only the building of wisdom and intuitional understanding by mutual effort can bind two souls by the laws of universal divine love, which is unconditional and has its foundation in service on the spiritual planes.

Friendship is the purest of all love. In the love of parents for their children there is compulsion; in filial love there is compulsion; in the love of lovers there is compulsion; but in true friendship there is no compulsion. Usefulness is love. If you want the love of friends or the world, you must be useful to them.

Be a Friend to Enemies

You must be a friend even to your enemy, because if you become an enemy to your enemy you will increase his wrath and make him an even greater enemy. Every person who tries to injure others, first injures himself. You cannot hate others without first poisoning yourself. To hate anyone is against your own interest.

Remember, God is in your enemy just as much as in your friend. When you recognize God in those who love you and in those who hate you, when you see the all-pervading love of God, then you will realize His omnipresence.

Hatred travels through the ether. If someone is broadcasting hatred, and you are tuned to that hatred, you will get it; but if you are tuned to love, no matter how many hateful vibrations are sent, you will not get them. You must cultivate love in your heart, for love is the magnet that draws souls to you and it is the dagger that destroys hatred.

In pure friendship you will find God. If you would be a true friend, you must recognize the soul. When you consider yourself as a soul, then you can be a perfect friend. If you fail to be friendly, you disregard the divine law of self-expansion by which alone your soul can grow into Spirit. By being true to yourself and a true friend to others, you gain the friendship of God.

THE DIVINE PURPOSE OF FRIENDSHIP

Friendship is the universal spiritual attraction that unites souls in the bond of divine love. The Spirit was One. By the law of duality it became two—positive and negative. Then, by the law of infinity applied to the law of relativity, it became many. Now the One in the many is endeavoring to unite the many and make them one. This effort of the Spirit, to unify many souls into the One, works through our emotions, intelligence, and intuition, and finds expression through friendship.

FRIENDSHIP

Is friendship the weaving of the red strings of two hearts?
Is it the blending of two minds into a spacious one-mind?
Is it the spouting of love founts together—
To strengthen the rush of love on droughty souls?
Is it the one rose grown 'twixt twin mind-branchlets
Of one compassionate stem?

Is it the one thinking in two bodies?
Or, is it like two strong stallions,
Disparate in color and mien,
Pulling the chariot of life together
To the single goal with one mind sight?
Is friendship founded on equalities or inequalities?
Is it built on diverse stones of differences?
Is friendship the unthinkingly agreeing,
The hand in hand, blind walking of two souls,
Foolishly rejoicing in their united folly,
Falling at last into pits of disillusionment?

Friendship is noble, fruitful, holy—
When two separate souls march in difference
Yet in harmony, agreeing and disagreeing,
Glowingly improving diversely,
With one common longing to find solace in true pleasure.
When ne'er the lover seeks
Self-comfort at cost of the one beloved,
Then, in that garden of selflessness

Fragrant friendship perfectly flowers.
For friendship is a hybrid, born of two souls,
The blended fragrance of two unlike flowers
Blown together in love's caressing breeze.
Friendship is born from the very core
Of secret, inexplicable likings.
Friendship is the fountain of true feelings.
Friendship grows in both likeness and difference.
Friendship sleeps or dies in familiarity,
And decays in lusts of narrow-eyed selves.
Friendship grows tall and sturdy
In the soil of oneness in body, mind, and soul.
Demands, deceptions, sordid sense of possession,
Courtesy's lack, narrow self-love, suspicion,
These are cankers which eat at the heart of friendship.
Ah, friendship! Flowering, heaven-born plant!
Nurtured art thou in the soil of measureless love,
In the seeking of soul-progress together
By two who would smooth the way each for the other.
And thou art watered by attentions of affection

And the tender dews of inner and outer sweetness
Of the inmost, selfless heart's devotion.
Ah, friendship! Where thy soul-born flowers fall—
There, on that sacred shrine of fragrance,
The Friend of all friends craves to come and remain!

The Friendship Instinct

God's effort to unite strife-torn humanity manifests itself within your heart as the friendship instinct.

Make every effort to rediscover your friends of past incarnations, whom you may recognize through familiar physical, mental and spiritual qualities. Rising above considerations of material or even spiritual gain, perfect your friendship, begun in a preceding incarnation, into divine friendship.

When divine friendship reigns supreme in the temple of your heart, your soul will merge with the vast Cosmic Soul, leaving far behind the confining bonds which separated it from all of God's animate and inanimate creation.

Chapter 2

THE FOLLY OF SELFISHNESS

JUDGMENT

Whenever you talk against another person for the love of gossip or through force of habit, remember, you will be judged by your Heavenly Father in the same way. Whatever you give out, the same will you attract. If you peddle the weaknesses of others, the Divine Law will mysteriously bring about the publicity of your own inner faults.

Gossip never heals the person talked about; it only makes him angry, or steeped in despair and ashamed. It strengthens his determination to continue to be evil. There is a proverb which says: "The man who has lost one ear goes through the village at the side, showing the villagers his best ear, and hiding the lost ear. But he who has lost both ears, goes through the center of the village, because he cannot hide from anyone."

Any person whose moral errors are unduly exposed becomes desperate and shameless, like the man who lost both ears, and thus he makes no effort to be better. That is why you must not judge in a way to harm the person judged.

"Judge ye not others; judge yourself." If you love to talk loudly about the faults of others, then satisfy that lust by loudly talking about your own secret faults, and see how you like it even for a minute. If you cannot stand one minute's publicity about your own faults, then you must not rejoice in exposing others.

The evil you spread about others becomes exaggerated, and people are ready to crucify the condemned person without knowing the circumstances that led him to be morally weak. Of course, in rare cases, the fear of publicity keeps some people good, but publicity about a person's fault makes him lose the desire to be good. Also, through publicity, a little weakness in a person is made to seem big, whereas people with far greater weaknesses go unnoticed.

If there is mental dirt in your own inner home, get busy and clean it out and do not waste time in talking about the mental dirt existing in others. Those who are self-elected critics are usually the ones who forget to scrutinize their own inner weaknesses. They think that they are all right because they can perceive the faults of others. Do not hide behind such an erroneous mental smoke screen. Unless you are free from fault yourself, you have no right to tell others how to be free from the very faults that haunt you.

Only a kind, wise, and perfectly poised person is in a position to tell others their faults. According to the law of cause and effect, if you judge others with kindness, you will receive the same treatment from the principle of

Truth, which secretly governs all life. If you judge others unkindly, you will attract adverse criticism from others, which will make you miserable.

To reveal the weakness of others, causing them embarrassment and making them resentful, is not wise. Cruel judgment of the wrong actions of others makes one forget that the sinner is only an error-stricken child of God. You should hate the sin but not the sinner, for he is your own divine brother whose understanding is eclipsed by ignorance. The purpose of judgment must be curative only, not the merciless outlet of anger. We should treat the error-stricken person as we would like to be treated if we ourselves were stricken with error. In the same spirit with which we judge others does the divine law judge us.

UNKINDNESS

Unkind words are ruthless murderers of life-long friendships and of the harmony of homes. Banish unkind words from your lips forever, and make your home life safe from trouble. Sincere, sweet words are nectar to thirsty souls.

Make yourself attractive by wearing the fine garment of genuine courteous language. First, be courteous to your immediate relatives. When you can do that, you will be habitually kind to all people. Real family happiness has its foundation on the altar of understanding and kind words.

In order to be kind, it is not necessary to agree about everything, but if you do disagree, always remain calm and courteous. It is human weakness to get angry and scold, but it shows divine strength to be able to hold the reins of the wild steeds of your temper and speech. No matter what the provocation, behave yourself, and by calm silence, or by genuine kind words, show that your kindness is more powerful than the other person's ugliness. Before the mellow light of your forgiveness all the gathered hatred of your enemies will melt away.

OVER-SENSITIVITY

Sensitiveness is due to lack of control over the nervous system. Sometimes a thought runs through the mind and the nerves rebel against that thought. Even if there is a reason for being upset, one should not become touchy or excited. If you feel that there is a reason to be upset and yet you control yourself, then you are master of yourself.

We should not be touchy or have self-pity, which increases our over-sensitivity. You may be nursing a grievance about something and nobody knows what it is. It is best that you look within yourself to remove the cause of that sensitiveness.

Many people think that they should pity themselves and that self-pity will bring a little relief, but self-pity is an addiction like opium. Every time the opium addict takes the drug, he becomes more and more steeped in the habit. Be as firm as steel against self-pity.

You must be able to control your moods instantly. If the fire of sensitiveness eats into your heart and you allow it to stay there, it eats into the fibers of your peace. You must be able to control it yourself, knowing that over-sensitivity is nothing but an agent of Satan trying to destroy your peace. Every time sensitiveness visits your heart, it is static on the radio of your soul and disconnects you from the divine song of peace that might play within you if you were not over-sensitive. Whenever sensitiveness comes, try to conquer your emotion, and do not blame others. Take responsibility for it yourself. That is the way to get rid of it.

DESTRUCTIVE CRITICISM

There are two kinds of criticism: constructive and destructive. When criticism is administered to people who resent your correction, that is destructive criticism. Constructive criticism consists in giving soul-awakening advice to friends who want and have asked for your help. Constructive criticism is given in a loving way.

It is not easy to criticize others accurately and kindly until you know that you can first criticize yourself perfectly. When you can clearly picture the faults of others and look at those faults with a sympathetic attitude, as if they were your own, then you are correct in your criticism.

Internal criticism is worse than criticism by words. It is very foolish to criticize others internally and silently. Clean your mind of all adverse criticism toward others.

Use a look to criticize others lovingly, use a hint to criticize lovingly, and use as few words as possible to criticize others if they want your criticism. Do not repeat your suggestion more than twice. Leave your loving criticism as a seed to germinate in the soil of recipient souls. If they want to cultivate those seeds, it is their privilege. You can't force others to do what you want them to do. By correct criticism at the right time, you can help people to a great extent.

When the scales of ignorance fall away from your inner eyes, you will be able to exactly measure the good points and the difficulties of others. You will not only learn to be tolerant, but you will learn to worship only what is good and to be indifferent to what is psychologically unwholesome.

We forgive ourselves under all circumstances. Why should we not forgive others under all circumstances? When we are in error, we do not like to advertise our faults, but when anyone else is in error, we like to advertise his or her faults right away. When divine love possesses your heart, then you become a divine critic. A divine critic is a healer who has courage to undertake the unpleasant responsibility of correcting his own children, with only one object in view—to make them better.

JEALOUSY

If you are a naturally homely woman and are jealous of naturally beautiful women, then adopt all the reasonable beauty-parlor tricks to make yourself attractive. Better than that: if your body is ugly, decorate your soul with the richest ornaments of sincerity, magnetic personality, intoxicating and contagious smiles, rare culture, and all-round efficiency to suit the demands and temperament of the most fastidious person.

Remember what makes you really beautiful. Beautiful bodies with worthless souls are nothing but skeletons hiding behind the smooth sepulcher of flesh. To live and act as if you have no soul is equal to being dead.

If you are jealous of another's fleshly accouterments, carry on continuous disciplinary inner practice until you bedeck your soul with the all-alluring spiritual qualities of an advanced soul. Beautify your countenance with an all-winning, melancholy-dissolving smile. Don the smile that comes from a clear conscience, right action, harmlessness, and inner and outer agreeableness.

If you are jealous of another person's health as compared to your own poor health, then try your utmost to follow all the laws of health with scrutiny, patience, and perseverance, until you are very healthy.

Jealousy is constructive as well as destructive. When jealousy is constructive and a harbinger of beneficial results, then it is good. If you are jealous of your better business rival to the point that you direct your efforts in channels of accelerated activity toward the attainment of greater success, that can be beneficial. But, unless due precaution is taken, constructive jealousy might be metamorphosed into destructive jealousy. Destructive jealousy is mean and seeks to jeopardize the interests of the jealous individual as well as the object of his jealousy.

FLATTERY VS. TRUTH

It is always good to speak the truth, but it is better to speak pleasant truth and avoid unpleasant true utterances. To address a lame man: "Hey, Mr. Lame Man," may be true, but it is an unpleasant and harmful truth and should be avoided. It is bad to criticize when criticism is not wanted, but it is beneficial to *listen to* kind criticism, and it is admirable to be able to stand harsh but true criticism with a smile and a sense of grateful appreciation.

Flattery may be good when it encourages a person to right action, yet it is pernicious when it serves to hide a spiritual wound and lets it fester and poison the soul with ignorance. We all love flattery, just as many people would unknowingly eat poisoned honey. We also love inwardly to excuse our harmful faults and hide big psychological boils that can break and poison our spiritual life.

Flattery from others and the comforting whispers of our own thoughts strike sweetly on our sense of hearing. Our human wisdom is often held prisoner in the hands of poisonous flattering words. Many people willingly lose money, time, health, and even character for the sweet, deceptive words of parasitic, so-called friends.

A saint used to have a friend who constantly criticized him, to the great displeasure of his disciples. One day a disciple came to him exulting: "Master, your enemy, the constant fault finder, is dead." The master began to weep and said: "My best spiritual critic is dead. My heart is broken."

Most people choose flattery instead of intelligent criticism, and would readily dash themselves on the rocks to disprove the candid forecasts of frank spiritual teachers. Therefore, each time somebody mildly or harshly criticizes you, ask yourself: "Have I been lured by sweet words and allowed my wisdom to be carried away a prisoner in the hands of flattery?"

Remember

You can't love God and at the same time be unkind to your associates. You can't love Him and be full of wrath. How you behave toward others both reflects your inner consciousness and conditions it.

Never imagine that you can win God's love if you can't win the love of your fellow creatures. As you love Him, so should you love Him in all.

O Fountain of Love, make us feel that our hearts and our love for our dear ones are all flooded by Thy Omnipresent Love. O Great Source of the rivers of our desires, teach us not to run ourselves dry or lose ourselves in the sands of short-lived sense-satisfactions. Bless us that the rivulets of all our sympathy, affection, and love, lose not themselves in the drought of dreary selfishness.

Chapter 3

HOW TO BE A FRIEND

SERVICE IS THE KEYNOTE OF FRIENDSHIP

Cultivate true friendliness, for only thus do you attract true friends to yourself. True friendship consists in being mutually useful, in offering your friends good cheer in distress, sympathy in sorrow, advice in trouble, and material help in times of real need. Friendship consists in rejoicing in the good fortune of your friends and sympathizing with them in adversity. Friendship gladly foregoes selfish pleasures or self-interest for the sake of a friend's happiness, without consciousness of loss or sacrifice, and without counting the cost.

Never be sarcastic to a friend. Do not flatter him unless it is to encourage him. Do not agree with him when he is wrong. Real friendship cannot witness with indifference the false, harmful pleasure of a friend. This does not mean that you must quarrel. Suggest mentally, or if your advice is asked, give it gently and lovingly. Fools fight. Friends discuss their differences.

There are people who do not trust anyone and who utterly doubt the possibility of ever having true friends. Some, in fact, actually boast that they get along without friends. If you fail to be friendly, you disregard the divine law of self-expansion, by which alone your soul can grow into the Spirit. No man who fails to inspire confidence in other hearts, who is unable to extend the kingdom of his love and friendliness into other soul territories, can hope to spread his consciousness over Cosmic Consciousness. If you cannot conquer human hearts, you cannot conquer the Cosmic Heart.

THE IMPORTANCE OF ENVIRONMENT

Environment and the company you keep are of paramount importance. Your outer environment, in conjunction with your inner environment, through your habits, controls your life and molds your tastes and habits. Environmental troubles are born because of your conscious or unconscious actions in the past. You must blame yourself for that but not develop an inferiority complex about it. Trials do not come to destroy you, but that you may appreciate God better. God does not send those trials—they are born of your own making. All you have to do is to resurrect your consciousness from the environment of ignorance.

Remember that the inner mental environment of an individual is what God judges. One may be a sinner at heart while living in the company of saints, or he may be a saint in the company of transgressors. Sinners or saints are largely made through the company they keep. If a sinner is willing to mend his ways and lives in the company of saints, he is bound to change, while a careless spiritual man will deteriorate in the company of wicked people. Through reaction to our outer environment, from early childhood on, our inner mental environment is formed. This inner mental environment of thought and mental habits almost automatically guides our actions.

Secret to a Happy Environment

If you want to be loved, start loving others who need your love. If you want others to sympathize with you, start showing sympathy to those around you. If you want to be respected, you must learn to be respectful to everyone, both young and old. Remember, whatever you want others to be toward you, first be that yourself, then you will find others responding in like manner to you.

It is easy to wish that others would behave perfectly toward you, and it is easy to see their faults, but it is very difficult to conduct yourself properly and to consider your own faults. If you can remember to behave rightly, others will try to follow your example. If you can find your own faults without developing an inferiority complex, and can keep busy correcting yourself, you will be using your time more profitably than if you spent it in just wishing others to be better. Your good example will do more to change others than your wishing, your holy wrath, or your words.

The more you improve yourself, the more you will elevate others around you. The happier you become, the happier will be the people around you.

SELFISHNESS: GOOD AND EVIL

Let your supreme goal be to make others happy in order to gain happiness for yourself. Never pride yourself in the thought that you are acting unselfishly. Always think that you are doing things for your own pleasure, that you find your own highest pleasure in making others happy. You cannot teach the principles of unselfishness to others unless you first practice "selfish" generosity in your own life.

Whatever you do attracts those conditions to yourself. If you set an example of selfishness, people will behave selfishly toward you. Self-preservation is an instinct, but God gave you memory, intelligence, and imagination to understand the difficulties of others. Find happiness in helping whomever crosses your path.

Avoid evil selfishness, which is the root of all troubles, whether individual or national. First came bows and arrows to protect one selfishness against another selfishness. Then guns were invented, then machine guns, and now poisonous gases to protect the selfishness of one group of people against the selfishness of another group. There will be more suffering before mankind realizes that national selfishness is just as evil as personal selfishness

Your greatest security lies in the good will of others. If you are enthroned in the hearts of every one, that is the greatest kingship. If there are one hundred people in a town and each person is trying to take from the other, each one has ninety-nine enemies, but if each one is trying to help the other, then each will have ninety-nine friends.

Jesus gave up his body for all, and yet he is enjoying eternal life. In being wholly self-giving he was looking after his spiritual welfare.

World Family

You must remember that you are a part of the world family and cannot exist without it. You must think of others when thinking of your own needs. It is wrong to think only of yourself, excluding all others. A nation is built of small communities, and they are built of individuals. Even if you have an enemy, you must remember that he is your neighbor. Everyone is our own, for God is our Father and we are his children.

If you think only of the welfare of your hands and feet and fail to look after your head, your brain will not serve you well. You must supply the needs of the entire body. So it is that the brains, or leaders, of nations must work harmoniously with the hands and feet, or laborers, of nations. If they are divided, there will be disorder and suffering.

We really do not own anything. We shall have to part with everything sometime, either by accident, theft, deterioration, or death. We are only given the use of things for a while. When something is given to you, you must know that it is only yours for a little while. You must not become attached to it. In time, your loved ones will be taken away from you. They were just given to you that you might learn to sacrifice for others and share with others.

The true Self is the manifestation of Spirit within. Anything that you do for the Self could be called "Selfishness." Good Selfishness consists of those actions by which the pure image of the Self within can be realized. Evil selfishness is that which you do for the ego, thus going against the true interest of the Self.

"Love God with all your heart," and "Love your neighbor as yourself." You will need no other commandments if you follow these two.

How to Convert Enemies into Friends

Practice loving those who do not love you. Feel for those who do not feel for you. Be generous to those who are generous only to themselves. If you heap hatred on your enemy, neither he nor you are able to perceive the inherent beauty of your soul.

You need not fawn on your enemy. Silently love him. Silently be of service to him whenever he is in need, for love is real only when it is useful and expresses itself through action. Thus will you rend the veils of hate and of narrow-mindedness that hide God from your sight.

If humility and apologies on your part bring out your enemy's good qualities, by all means apologize. The person who can do this will have attained a definite spiritual development, for it takes character to be able to apologize graciously and sincerely. It is the consciousness of his own inferiority that makes a man hide behind a display of pride. Do not, however, encourage a wrong doer by being inappropriately humble and apologetic. Take his actual realities into account. Be practical in your idealism.

Finding Friends of Past Incarnations.

There are people with whom you come in contact daily, yet with whom you do not feel in sympathy. Learn to love them and adapt yourself to them. There are others who give you the instantaneous feeling that you have known them always. This indicates that they are your friends of previous incarnations. Do not neglect them; strengthen the friendship existing between you. Be on the lookout for them always, as your restless mind may fail to recognize them. Often they are very near you, drawn by the friendship born in the distant past. They constitute your shining collection of soul jewels; add to it constantly. In these bright soul galaxies you will behold the one Great Friend smiling at you radiantly and clearly. It is God who comes to you in the guise of a noble, true friend, to serve, inspire, and guide you.

Ugliness of disposition and selfishness drive away all friends of former incarnations, whereas friendliness draws them toward you. Therefore, be ready always to meet them halfway. Never mind if one or two friends prove false and deceive you.

Each individual has his own standard of physical and mental beauty. What seems ugly to one may appear beautiful to another. Looking at a vast crowd, you like some faces immediately; others do not attract you particularly. The instant attraction of your mind to the likeable inner and outer features of an individual is your first indication that you have found a friend of the past. Your dear ones whom you loved before will be drawn toward you by a prenatal sense of friendship.

Do not be deceived by physical beauty; ask yourself whether or not the face, the manner of walking—in short, everything about a person—appeals to you. Sometimes overeating and lack of exercise may distort the features of a friend, and thus he may escape your recognition. Sometimes a beautiful woman may fall in love with an ugly man, or a handsome man, with a physically unattractive woman, due to the loving friendship of a past incarnation.

To be sure that your eyes have not deceived you regarding the physical characteristics of your supposed former friend, ascertain whether you are mentally and spiritually congenial. Delve deeply into a person's mind, and guard yourself against being prejudiced by little peculiarities, in order to find out whether your tastes and inclinations essentially agree. Seek your friends of past incarnations in order that you may continue your friendship in this life and perfect it into Divine Friendship. One lifetime is not always sufficient to achieve such perfection.

When you behold, assembled all at once beneath the canopy of your perfected universal friendship, souls of the past, present, and future, the busy stars, the whippoorwill, the dumb stones, and the shining sea sands, then the friendship thirst of your heart will be quenched forever. Then God's creation will ring with the emancipating song of all-difference-dissolving celestial friendship. Then the Divine Friend will rejoice to see you come home after your evolutional wanderings through the pathways of incarnations. Then He and you will merge in the bliss of eternal friendship.

Heavenly Father! Let those that are our own come unto us, and finding them may we find friendship with all, and thus find Thee.

Expand Your Love to All

Relatives are those whom we think of as our own. To love our relatives trains us in expanding our consciousness, and helps us practice loving all people as our relatives in God. For relatives and strangers are all equally God's children. If you limit your love to your own direct family, you have Christ consciousness to only that limited degree. When you love your neighbors as your wider family, you express more of Christ consciousness. When you feel for all people with the love that you feel for your own loved ones, then you are expressing Christ consciousness more fully.

Wherever there is a lonely heart or a weeping brother by the wayside, and your heart goes out to that soul, you have expanded your consciousness toward true, infinite Christ consciousness.

My Master [Sri Yukteswar] once asked me, "Do you love people?" I answered, "No, I love only God."

"That isn't enough," he replied.

Later he asked me again, "Do you love people?"

This time, I smiled blissfully and said, "Don't ask me." He could see that my love, now, was too broad to be spoken about. This time, he only smiled.

SELFLESS LOVE

When you are one with the Infinite, you aren't aware of yourself as an ego; you only know that the wave of life could not work and dance without the ocean behind it. If you become too much attached to the things of this life, you will forget God. That is why we lose things—not to punish us, but to see if we love littleness more than Infinity.

In order to develop spiritually, you must first follow the universal spirit of Christ. This doesn't mean that you have to be crucified in order to be like Christ! Still, all useless desires must, in a sense, be crucified. Some people seek the gifts of God, but those who are wise seek God, the Giver of all gifts. You may try to please people, but after a while they will forget you. A statue might be erected in your honor, but few will look at it and remember your good deeds.

Sociability must be developed, but that doesn't mean that you need to know everyone personally and individually. You must invite the whole world into your heart. Christ consciousness encompasses everything in its love. That consciousness was born in the body of Jesus, and in the body of other great masters. Until you have attained that consciousness, never judge anyone. With that consciousness, your judgment will always be kindly, and will, in fact, be simply an appraisal.

The Call of Friendship

God lives and breathes in all. We are Americans or have some other nationality for just a few years, but we are God's children forever. The soul cannot be confined within man-made boundaries. Its nationality is Spirit. Its country is Omnipresence.

First, love your family as you love yourself. The greatest impulse is to love oneself only, but as soon as you can love someone else as much as, or even more than, yourself, you have advanced spiritually. To the extent that you love yourself more than anyone else, to that extent are you enclosed in your own ego.

If you wish to develop, you must go through three stages: You must love your family more than yourself, your nation as you love your own family, and the world, finally, as you love your own nation.

By being true to yourself, and a true friend to others, you will gain the friendship of God. If you are not friendly toward them, you disregard the divine law of self-expansion by which alone your soul can grow into Spirit. Anyone who fails to inspire confidence in other hearts, who is unable to extend the kingdom of his love and friendliness into other soul territories, cannot hope to expand his consciousness into Cosmic Consciousness.

True friendship unites souls so completely that they reflect the unity of Spirit and its divine qualities. When divine friendship reigns supreme in the temple of your heart, your soul will merge with the vast Cosmic Soul, leaving far behind the confining bonds which separate it from all of God's animate and inanimate creation.

A MEDITATION ON EXPANDING LOVE

Tell yourself: "My kingdom of love must expand. I have loved my body more than anything else. That is why I am identified with and limited by it. With the love that I have for this body, I will love all those who love me. With the expanded love of those who love me, I will love those who are mine. With the love for myself and the love for my own, I will love those who are strangers. I will use all my love to love those who do not love me, as well as those who love me. I will bathe all souls in my unselfish love. In the sea of my love, my family members, my countrymen, all nations, and all creatures will swim. All creation, all the myriads of tiny living things, will dance on the waves of my love!"

Chapter 4

SPIRITUAL MARRIAGE AND FAMILY LIFE

Creating a Spiritual Marriage

How to Select Your Life Companion

When selecting your life partner, you must understand the impulses that influence you. You are subject to the following influences:

1. Physical attraction
2. Aesthetic attraction
3. Mental affinity
4. Vocational similarity
5. Moral inclinations
6. Affinity of ideals
7. Emotional liking
8. Material greed
9. Attraction to social position
10. Call of the soul.

Many young couples get married because they have certain similar mental traits. Mental unity *is* one of the indications of proper mating in matrimony, but it is not everything. Mental unity may wear off if there is no inner unity.

One young man says: "I like her because she loves to watch football games, as I do. I love her because she loves to smoke, drink, and dine as I do. I love her because she loves the movies and reads detective stories, even as I do." Another says: "I love her because she likes music and poetry and business, as I do."

Some couples get married because they like the same kind of work. He says: "I am a movie actor. I love her because she is a movie actress."

In modern times it is extremely important to have a partner who is interested in the development of your business. Doctors and lawyers should not marry jealous partners, who might become jealous of their patients and clients.

Men of genius should not marry super-intelligent women, for quarrels are apt to result. Such a man might be jealous of any superiority of intelligence he finds in his mate.

Some men prefer good looking, obedient, ignorant, and adoring young wives. Other youthful couples marry because they are attracted by good looks, but most people who marry for beauty alone soon part. Physical beauty, if it is not supported by beautiful mental qualities, is the first thing to pall. After the infatuation of beauty passes, the most beautiful face may begin to seem ugly.

What people get, they often do not want; what they want, they often do not get. Of course, personal beauty has its place in the plan of life, but greater than physical beauty is mental beauty. Souls that are dressed in purity, appareled with sweet speech, dressed in wisdom, and accustomed to unending, unconditional love, exercise a lasting magnetic hold on their mates.

Never Marry for Money or Social Position

Some men like to marry rich widows and some women like to choose rich bachelors, but marriage for money never lasts, and usually ends in the accusation: "You married me for my money!" Those who want money should go into business and earn it; they should never try to get rich quick through marriage. There is life-long humiliation in store for the man who marries a woman for her money. And, one wife said: "I married a rich man all right, but he is the worst husband; he beats me whenever I spend money even for bare necessities."

Many couples marry for social position. Don't try to climb into society through marriage. Gain money and fame by developing your own usefulness and you will automatically attract social prominence. Don't try to become famous by basking in the halo of somebody else's fame.

Do Not Marry Under the Stress of Emotion

Some young couples marry because they love to do things in an excited state. They indulge in meteoric marriages and meteoric divorces. Some people want to get married for the thrill of tasting the forbidden fruit. One rich American girl ran away with the family chauffeur, and when the thrill of resisting her father's will was over, she fled from her husband—immediately after the honeymoon!

Two couples once actually suggested that I marry them as the five of us floated down in parachutes from 15,000 feet above sea level! I declined the offer. They wanted only to marry for the thrill of the publicity. They'd have gotten divorced after the publicity stunt and the excitement had passed. I said: "But why go to that expense?" The answer was: "Oh, we will spend anything for adventure and front-page publicity."

The second reason I declined to perform this bizarre marriage ceremony while jumping from a plane was, as I told them: "Well, if the parachutes fail to open, I shall be performing the marriage ceremony in heaven with broken skeletons." High school boys and girls usually like to marry under the influence of a somewhat similar kind of excitement.

Love for Sense Pleasures

The devotee, trying to delve deep into soul happiness, is often suddenly possessed by his subconscious habitual love for the sense-pleasures. At that time, all the golden hopes of eternal happiness, pictured by his inner wisdom, seem as if empty and useless. Then the devotee thinks: "If I have to forsake tangible earthly happiness now, there is no use in gaining anything, no matter how beautiful the promise of future happiness."

The devotee, in extreme sympathy with his sense desires, begins to think: "I would rather not be armed with self-control and with the power to resist evil, and let my spiritual happiness be slain by the weapons of temptation, than be involved in a devastating battle between my discriminative forces and my sense-pleasures."

No devotee should use such false reasoning. Never try to deceive your soul with the fear of renouncing familiar but inferior sense-pleasures for superior, but-yet-to-be-acquired, soul bliss. Every devotee, instead of being despondent, should be glad to consign inferior sense-pleasures to oblivion in exchange for the unending pleasures of the soul.

Simply say "No!" therefore. Don't try to reason your way out of temptation. No doubt you've already done as much reasoning as is needed to persuade your *conscious* mind that soul joy is superior to sensory pleasure. What you must deal with now is your *subconscious* mind. To do this, be strongly affirmative. Reason, at this point, will be your undoing.

CREATING A LASTING MARRIAGE

Give serious thought before deciding to marry. Do not marry until you are sure that your marriage will be enduring. Young people should not touch or kiss one another until they are sure, first, of their unity on a soul level. Many youthful couples fall in love and marry while blinded by physical attraction. Then, when the fog of passion clears away, they see their partner's true nature and may actually become disgusted. Like shuttlecocks, they fly into the divorce courts.

When husbands and wives lose mutual respect due to the deterioration of their moral standards, they cease to love each other. If young people continuously develop their moral standards after marriage, they will remain married because of the regard developed in moral emulation.

Many couples marry because they each have lofty ideals and because together they want to preach, teach, and inspire other people. Sometimes, if the wife is respected more by her followers, then the husband becomes jealous, and vice versa.

Husbands and wives must both develop their love for true ideals, then their love will continually increase, until the love of their hearts burns as a single divine flame. If the husband desecrates his idealism before the idealistic eyes of his wife, then he will lose her love. When idealism is the spring of love, if idealism dries, the fountain of love will suffer drought. Married couples who continuously become more idealistic at home, in society, and in the world, find their love ever growing and changing, until that love becomes the idealistic love of God.

Seek Complete Unity

Young people should consult real spiritual advisors before they marry, and should be guided by long, well-tested courtship experiences. Before they marry they should, first and foremost, find out whether their unity is on a soul level.

Real soul marriage consists in an inborn, undying, unconditional mutual liking, which may be felt at first sight, or may be the result of protracted divine companionship and courtship. In soul union, unconditional love between married couples grows deeper and deeper.

There is a supernatural affinity between kindred souls. As positive and negative currents join to light an incandescent lamp, so also a perfect, positive soul combined with a perfect negative (receptive) soul become fused into the light of ever growing love. Soul love must take the place of animal love. Soul harmony must be the spring of action in marriage.

True marriage is only for people who seek divine love in human expression. This is very difficult, for almost all marriages are preceded by only a little love, with passion predominating. In such cases, sex takes the place of love. Then true love, which is unconditional, quickly slips from the heart. On the other hand, if love increases, and physical consciousness decreases, then human love evolves into divine love. Thus, both souls realize that they did not love each other as bodies, but loved God alone through their outward illusion of human love.

Human love in marriage can never last unless its purpose is to express divine love. Without divine love, married couples fail to entertain or respect one another, and the marriage goes on the rocks. Sex charm, intellectuality, beauty, money, culture, or personal magnetism cannot keep two souls together. Every man and woman seeks perfect love in his or her mate, but it is impossible of fulfillment until divine love is expressed in action, motive, and in all life's ambitions.

The Power of Magnetism

Magnetism is a drawing, uplifting, expanding power. Magnetic power is a quality of the Spirit. We hear someone say: "Oh, I met a friend who is so magnetic that he inspired me, and expanded my consciousness." This is the magnetic power that we all want. This power expands the consciousness, unlike hypnosis or animal magnetism, which merely stupefies it.

Every mother should teach her daughter to attract others by spiritual magnetism only, and to be dressed with the real magnetic qualities of wisdom, understanding, thoughtfulness, presence of mind, true learning, and all-round efficiency. Spiritual magnetism will draw spiritual souls.

When Marriage Is Unnecessary

Better than marriage, or ineffectually trying to weld unsuited souls together, is the unity between a soul and God. The more we allow ourselves to be drawn toward matter, the more our souls will express disharmony and unhappiness. When, however, the love-starved, joy-starved, complete-satisfaction-starved soul turns toward the perfect, all-loving, blissful God, then a real spiritual marriage results. God is the Bridegroom, and all souls are His brides.

Marriage is unnecessary for those who are wedded to the ever-intoxicating bliss God. That is why Jesus, St. Francis,

Swami Shankara, and Babaji were unmarried. They had found perfect love, perfect joy, and a perfect mate in the complete and perfect God—hence they had no need to marry.

Marriage is a delusive way of finding God. In the moonlight, under the influence of passion and emotion, married couples promise each other eternal love. When they die, the moon laughs at their skulls strewn in graves over the earth. It laughs, reflecting on their failed promises, given under the intoxication of emotion.

God is the only one who fulfills His promise of loving us eternally. Hence, union of the soul with the Cosmic Beloved should be the highest goal of every soul. Union with God will bring perfect love and perfect, eternal fulfillment, free from the disappointments that attend all lesser fulfillments.

How to Avoid Mistakes

The spiritual way to choose the right companion is to affirm deeply after meditation: "Heavenly Father, bless me that I choose my life companion according to Thy law of perfect soul union."

If you practice this affirmation for six months with deep faith, you will marry your right companion, or the Divine

Father will bring about sudden unfavorable circumstances which completely prevent your wrong marriage.

IDEAL LAWS OF MARRIED LIFE

Couples thinking of marrying should honestly test whether their natures harmonize or not, and whether their love can and will exist under all conditions during their natural social contact. They should find out whether their love has a foundation in real cooperation around a common ideal. Look for a partner who is in harmony with your moral beliefs, hereditary and present habits, business goals, tastes, inclinations, and spiritual aspirations.

Before marriage, expose your prospective husband or wife to your business and social activities informally, and find out whether he or she fits in with your habits and ideals. In the same way, explore whether you fit in with your partner's ambitions, temperament, and ideals.

The greatest secret of preserving matrimonial life lies in the art of self-control. Learn to love your wife or husband more on the spiritual plane, and associate with her or him as a close friend, without constantly focusing on the physical plane. If you can do that, you will win the greatest of all battles in keeping your spouse inwardly loyal, respectful, and loving toward you. Occasionally come together physically and feel it a privilege to do so; feel then that you are meeting your companion after ages of separation. Mingle with your whole heart, attention, and courtesy. When that deep attention begins to wear off, that is the time to stop.

Plan of Behavior for the Husband

The following rules should be obeyed by the ideal husband who wants to keep his wife loyal and loving:

- Do not remain in the same room with your wife all the time.

- Do not encroach upon your wife's independence.

- Do not disturb your wife when she is busy with important work or with her personal friends.

- Sleep, if possible, in separate rooms.

- Do not insult or be sarcastic with your wife at any time.

- Do not argue with your wife at any time, especially before others.

- Go out often with her alone, and frequently with your children as well, and talk with her about literature, music, and higher spiritual truths.

- Your life and experience with your wife must be that of daily constant progress in material, mental, and spiritual ways.

- Your experience with your wife must be that of increasing happiness.

- Keep your body like the body of an athlete; eat raw food often, and keep your wife away from kitchen work as much as possible.

- Make your home life simple and your spiritual life deep.

- Never lie to your wife.

- Never insult her parents.

- Study wholesome books and moral literature with her.

- Never use harsh language, but always, instead, use sweet language.

- Be chivalrous to your wife always, addressing her sweetly, with dignity and attention, and thanking her for every courtesy.

• Remember her birthday and your wedding anniversary. Frequently, offer her presents of things she needs, but not necessarily what appeals to her consciousness of luxury.

• Do not be jealous of your wife, nor make her life miserable with nagging. If you can't keep your wife's attention by love, nothing else will succeed in keeping it.

• Do not act as if you owned your wife. Help her feel that you are glad to have whatever she gives you from her soul.

• Give her freedom to choose her women friends. Learn to respect and, if possible, to like her friends.

• Live a simple, inexpensive life and inspire her to do the same. Save more; do not spend too much for luxuries.

• Meditate with your wife every morning and night—especially at night.

• Read the Bible and/or other spiritual books together.

• Offer devotion to God by chanting or singing together.

• Have a little family altar where you, your wife, and your children gather to offer deep devotion to God, that your souls may be united forever in ever-joyous cosmic consciousness.

Plan of Behavior for the Wife

In addition to cooperating with her husband in the ways described above, she should also follow these guidelines:

• Try to make him comfortable.

• Try to teach him self-control by love, and live with him on a higher moral plane, learned through spiritual studies.

• The more you meditate with him, the more he will like you.

• By your example, win him. Don't use force or harsh speech. Try to win him by your ideal life.

• Keep yourself beautiful and well dressed—just as you were when you first met him.

• Never speak ill of him to your women friends. Never ridicule him or find fault with him, especially not before his children, and not even in private.

• Teach him only through silence and love. Never speak to him with sarcasm.

• Keep him busy when he is at home by reading, writing, singing, chanting, or meditating with him.

• Make yourself more and more useful and interesting to him.

• Give him the right things to eat: more raw food, fewer pastries and sweets. Food has much to do with matrimonial happiness.

• If your husband wanders away morally, do not nag him or speak bitterly. If you happen to know of his weakness, do not cooperate with him on the physical plane until he reforms; exercise great love and kind attention, and reform him by your love.

• Affirm daily after meditation: "Father, keep me and my husband perfectly united in body, mind, and soul, and in ever-increasing happiness by Thy perfect law."

Thus, day-by-day, the ideal husband and wife will find ever greater unity and love on the mental and spiritual planes, and less so on the physical plane. Ultimately, they will find emancipation in God. In Him their souls will be united in the bond of ever-increasing joy, never to part again. Mentally finding God in their souls, they will be one with Him.

DIFFICULTIES IN MARRIAGE

Marriage is Nature's law for procreation, not only on the physical, but also on the mental, intellectual, and spiritual planes. Without remembering the highest purpose of marriage, a married couple can never find happiness. Too much familiarity, lack of courtesy, over-sexuality, suspicion, insults, arguing before children or guests, crankiness, and unloading your troubles and wrath on your mate must be abandoned. Remember, true marriage is a laboratory, in which the poisons of selfishness, bad temper, and bad behavior must be poured into the test tube of patience, and neutralized by the power of love and continuous good behavior.

It has been said that a man wants a woman until he is sure of her. One wife said to her indifferent husband: "Dear, why is it that you bought me candies and flowers and showered me with attention before our marriage, and now you don't give me anything?"

The husband, with a cigar in his mouth, coldly looked at his wife and replied: "Why, don't you know! Who do you think is crazy enough to feed the fish after he has caught it?!"

The above is very bad philosophy, for the indifferent husband chills the warm affection of his wife, and the inattentive wife makes her husband callous. Courtesy in remembering birthdays and other important days, and reviving old reminiscences of affection, must be continued throughout life. A small flower tinged with affection, or a word fragrant with kindness, can do much to patch up old wounds. Put on your best suit of kindness and proper behavior first of all with your own mate and children. Practice kindness at home, and you will win everybody else by your magnetic aura of kindness.

Jealousy in Married Life

Jealousy in married life is extremely pernicious. If you are unmarried, do not marry a person who shows a potential for insane jealousy toward you. Especially do not marry a jealous person if you are a doctor, minister, lawyer, or if you work in any other public profession. A jealous spouse is more occupied with imaginary apprehensions than with your business welfare or your psychological peace. Jealousy is self-love. It slowly eats away at the roots of real love.

Even if you are jealous of your mate, never show it. If a husband or wife is reasonably jealous to guard his or her mate from falling into the traps of designing people, it is all right, but when jealousy makes you lose your temper and converts you into a sort of ravening demon, then abhor that tendency in yourself as one influenced by the psychological inducements of Satan.

If you are jealous because your mate tries occasionally to explore the affections of others, give him a hint or a warning. If he doesn't listen, do not say anything. Don't be jealous, or angry, or demanding. Everyone has the right of free will—even to err. But if you think that he is a worthy peg on which to hang your life, then put on your own best clothes of behavior. Meditate more, and be extra nice, extra cheerful, extra forgiving, extra lenient, and extra magnetic toward him. Do not use physical force to draw the straying attention of your mate, but use the superior spiritual force of offering more love.

Even if your love is rejected, do not be ungracious. "Kill" him with kindness! Let him leave you (if he must) in kindness, ever regretting that he left you, rather than force him to leap eagerly away from your nagging, jealous presence as if escaping the plague. Couples who once thought that they loved each other should never mock their feelings by later hating each other under the instigation of jealousy. If your love experiment in matrimony proves unsuccessful, then bid each other farewell in a kindly, gentle spirit, as befits true children of God.

If jealousy is incurable, despite the offering of more courtesy, more trust, more kindness, and more love, then you should part in friendliness and mutual understanding, saying to each other: "We tried our utmost, but our matrimonial experiment did not succeed, so let us part."

Jealousy is never a cure for jealousy. Love is the best panacea for this malevolent, ugly psychological trait. If you hate jealousy in others and watch with abhorrence its devastating effects on others, then, by all means, refrain from wearing the mark of this peace-murdering, psychological virus, yourself.

How to Cure the Disease of Jealousy

If husbands and wives, instead of target practicing on each other with bullets of wrathful language and discourtesy, would try to entertain each other with the soul-solacing charm of kind words, they would create a new happiness in family life. Unkind behavior increases by arguments and disagreements.

Unless conjugal love has a spiritual basis it can never last. If husbands and wives are to live in friendship and harmony, they must be of spiritual service to each other. Newlyweds who forget that true love is based on unselfish mutual service and friendship soon come to a parting of the ways.

When two souls are ideally mated, their love becomes spiritualized and is registered in eternity as the one love of God.

Love will win, where jealousy will surely fail. If love can't save your wrecked love, don't bring in the demon of jealousy, which might well prove the ruin of you both. If your wife goes astray, and you kiss her good-bye with love and say: "Come back when you are good," then perhaps only one soul will be lost. But if you kill or otherwise condemn your unfaithful, erring wife, then two souls will be lost. Your wife commits spiritual suicide, and you might have to go to "the hot place on a very hot chair." Do you see how foolish jealousy is? It kills the very thing it professes to love. Jealousy is self-love. If you loved a woman truly, you could not destroy her love for you by pushing her into the grave with a bullet, and let her go to the Beyond loathing you through eternity.

If love can't hold your mate, jealousy never will. Husbands and wives who think they have succeeded in restraining their mates from straying into mischief, only succeed in imprisoning the bodies of their mates, with their souls ever marauding in the marsh of evil. Jealousy breeds deceit. Love fosters trust.

Let your spouse gradually try to rise from his or her errors with your knowledge rather than continuing to do evil, camouflaged behind the screen of double-dealing.

THE HIGH PURPOSE OF MARRIAGE

Spiritual marriage means union with God, soul, and spirit. Marriage is not a man-made law. It is God-made.

Man has abused the high purpose of marriage. Marriage means unity on the physical, mental, and spiritual planes. If you attract a person by spiritual magnetism, then you will meet your soul companion.

Unless human love is spiritualized, it will be a canker in your soul. Unless you are spiritually minded and your mate is the same, you can never be happy. Spiritual marriage means to marry your soul to the eternal love of God. Without God, marriage cannot succeed. The purpose of marriage is to know God, and to be together in God. Unfortunately, this truth has been forgotten.

When you have formed with a person a deep friendship that nothing can destroy, a friendship that has no compulsion in it and that increases constantly, you have found a true mate.

In woman, feeling is expressed uppermost, and in man, reason is expressed uppermost. In married life, women and men bring out the hidden feeling and reason in each other, thus becoming more perfect in themselves. Reason and feeling in man and woman should be balanced, like the softness of the flower and the strength of steel, both of which are divine qualities.

God's is a love greater than the combined love of all lovers who have ever loved. If you learn the higher forms of meditation, you can have true spiritual marriage: union with God, the most beautiful love of all. Remember, no marriage can achieve its true purpose unless the husband and wife seek God first together. In marriage, love also grows by service to each other. When a husband and wife serve each other with the eternal inspiration of God, that is true, spiritual marriage.

People who rise above the physical plane and continuously strengthen the love of their souls find their oneness in God. When the love of two persons burns as one flame, then it has intoxicating eternal qualities. That marriage which is lived in self-control and intense spiritual preparation becomes emancipated.

Man and woman should know that the germ of the Infinite is within them. If you cannot find a true soul companion, do not marry. If you have found God, you do not need a human marriage. It is better to remain single than to enter into a wrong marriage. Transmute matrimonial love into love divine, and bring back your consciousness from the sex plane to the plane of paradise.

You may unite your feeling and reason by giving yourself to humanity. By having a bigger family, you have the right not to have a smaller, more limited one. For all those who are unmarried and wish to remain so, their greatest duty in life is to serve humanity.

If you have no children of your own, adopt or teach the children of someone else, live an ideal life, and instill soul qualities into them. What you instill in the souls of children is imperishable. Anything you do that perpetuates your life, such as creative deeds, is, in a sense, your child. Thus fulfill your own true purpose in life.

Sex: Right Use of the Creative Force

SPIRITUALIZING AND TRANSMUTING CREATIVE FORCE

(The following is written with the sole purpose of developing moral character and self-control, restoring harmony in unhappy marriages, and preventing wrong marriages and divorces.)

The creative impulse is a fact. It is one of the strongest instincts and impelling forces implanted by Nature in the human body, to advance the propagation of the species. Nature silently takes revenge on those who misuse or trifle with her holy method of creation. "Fig-leaf consciousness," or shame regarding sexuality, throws a veil of unholiness on this creative principle and has brought a great deal of moral and material suffering into the world. This creative principle has a two-fold purpose—one of them holy, the other to keep humanity bound to delusion.

Directed toward those nerves which are embedded in the reproductive area, this instinct wants not only to create, but to enjoy, physically. Misuse of this creative power keeps one matter-bound, groveling in the sticky mud of the senses.

On the other hand, if this creative instinct is withdrawn from the lower part of the spine and raised through the spine to that point which is centered in the forehead between the two eyebrows, it begins to create "offspring" of spiritual realization. Married people, after creating one or two children, should learn how to commune and procreate spiritually.

Parents, if they want to create a spiritual child, should prepare their minds months in advance. During the time of coming together sexually, thoughts of invoking a noble soul into the temple of united sperm and ovum cells must predominate. During intercourse, thought should remain at the point between the eyebrows, directing the holy work of creation, and should not be allowed to flow downward to become identified with passion.

In married life, adultery is committed by living wholly on the physical plane. Such lives are punished by boredom, mutual dislike, and final separation. Adultery originated in converting the means of physical creation into an end in itself. The creative instinct is Nature's means for reproduction and should not be converted into a play with the senses. Husband and wife should consider their union as the union of nature and spirit, of knowledge and feeling sparks. Their union is meant principally for spiritual union and only incidentally for physical union.

Elderly couples should commune only on the spiritual plane, intoxicated with mutual, pure love, satisfying the physical craving by loving mentally. The ratio between love and physical indulgence is that the greater the love the less the physical craving, and vice versa. Husband and wife should feel love, and not the physical instinct, whenever they see each other—otherwise they march toward the pitfalls of boredom, dislike—amounting sometimes to hatred, and separation.

A husband should consider his wife a clean temple fit for creating and caring for new souls. That temple should be free from every unclean thought. The quality of the mental state of parents during intercourse is the magnetic force which draws a compatible kind of soul into the mother's body temple. Thoughts concentrated on the physical invite sensual souls.

The Hindu Scriptures say that, in the union of sperm and ovum, a life current is generated that serves as a door through which the soul enters. Good souls do not enter this door of life current if its vibrations are of low passion. They prefer to wait rather than take hasty rebirth in an undesirable place. All husbands and wives should remember to cooperate spiritually and mentally, as well as physically, to invite a sacred soul in the cell temple that they may create. Married people should invoke good souls to come and live with them.

To trifle with physical passion is to gamble away untold joys of life. The evanescent excitement in physical union is nothing compared to the bliss that comes from withdrawing this creative impulse into the brain for the procreation of spiritual and intellectual qualities, such as love, consideration, divine patience, sympathy, determination, enthusiasm, calmness, and realization.

In married life, respect and tolerance of each other's views lead to happiness. Married people should refrain from contradicting each other before others, and from quarreling between themselves over little things. Husbands and wives should never discuss their marital troubles with others.

Love cannot be wrested from one another, but can only be received as a spontaneous gift. Love grows in tolerance, forgiveness, and trust, and is diminished by jealousy. In distant closeness Love lives. In wrong familiarity it sleeps.

A husband and wife should be loyal to each other and try to make each other happy in every way. The spiritual wife should not forsake the unspiritual husband, nor should the spiritual husband forsake the unspiritual wife—they should try, as long as it is possible to do so, to influence and help each other.

How to Regulate the Creative Impulse

The creative impulse is Nature-born and as such is not man's fault. People who are unable to control Nature's powerful force for propagating the species are blamed by society, but are not taught the method of governing this instinct instead of being governed by it. Even a lifelong intellectual or medical study will not enable the student to control this instinct. Here are practical methods of self-control:

1. Eat little or no meat, and more raw vegetables, fruits, nuts, and proper meat substitutes.

2. Understand that the creative force can be used in four ways:

- It can be dissipated through sex, which is weakening and causes much disease and mental as well as physical debility.

- The creative energy can be used for the physical creation of a child.

- It can create spiritual "children," also, of wisdom and genius by converting creative energy into thought-power by sublimation and transmutation. One can engage his mind in creative work such as art, inventions, business, or literary work—whichever of these activities is most interesting to him. In this way, his creative energy will be rechanneled to the brain.

- One can also rechannel the creative energy into sports or strenuous physical exercise.

3. One can withdraw the energy upward from the sex organs toward the region of the medulla oblongata, through conscious use of the breath. Concentrate mentally on the generative area in the body, and inhale deeply and slowly, thinking of the breath as starting from that area. Imagine that you are redirecting the downward-flowing life energy upward, as you inhale. Imagine the breath flowing inward from the reproductive area, then upward through the spine to the point between the eyebrows. Hold breath and mind there at the point between the eyebrows, and mentally count one to twenty-five (or even longer), and think of yourself as absorbing all passion as you pour life-current into the reservoir of life-energy present in the medulla and at the point between the eyebrows. Then exhale and relax, freeing yourself from every vestige of passion.

Repeat the above method three times with closed eyes. During relaxation, think of the physical instinct as having been completely expelled from the body. At these times, do not seek solitude.

Such are the teachings of the great scriptures of India.

Hints to Married and Unmarried People

1. Realize the mind's intrinsic power over the body. Undesirable physical thoughts should be removed from the mind first, by diverting all one's thoughts to other interesting things.

2. The undesirable creative impulse should be regulated psychologically, first, and then physiologically. The attack on this impulse must be both from within and from without.

3. Avoid anything that, through the senses of sight, touch, etc., stimulates the sexual impulse.

4. Avoid dwelling on and discussing undesirable stories. Be unresponsive when someone tells a dirty story. Never feed your creative instinct unconsciously with degrading thoughts.

5. Try to understand the physiology of the reproductive organs by studying some standard medical book.

6. Boys and girls, men and women, should interact not with a physical consciousness, but with the thought of purity and holy friendship.

7. It is best for married people to dance only with their own spouses.

8. Moderation mixed with self-discipline and complete mastery over the creative impulse awakens the powers of spiritual perception. It is, indeed, the highest virtue. Marriage is meant for spiritual reunion of souls and not for physical license.

9. Those unmarried people who never break the law of celibacy create in themselves a powerful magnetism that draws a true soul companion, if they desire to marry. Others may attract wrong companions through the misguided creative instinct. Spiritual magnetism, if lost in wrong marriage or in unmarried life through indiscretion, can be revived by the practice of the Energization Exercises*, and by meditation.

10. Unmarried people can unite the creative-nature-force spiritually with the soul-force within them, by learning the right method of meditation and by applying it to physical life. They may not have to go through the experience of outer marriage, if they learn to marry their feminine physical impulse with the masculine soul force within.

In seeking their life companion, unmarried people should not depend wholly on their own inclinations, but

---

* Yogananda created a system of Energization Exercises for recharging the body with vital energy. For more information on these, contact the publisher.

should consult their parents, and, above all, persons of wisdom and intuitive insight.

DRAWING A SPIRITUAL CHILD

A couple expressed to me their desire for a spiritual child. I prayed for them, then showed them a photograph. This soul, I told them, would be suitable for them and was also, I felt, ready to be reborn on earth.

"Meditate on this soul," I said. "Concentrate especially on the eyes. Invite him to come dwell in your home. In addition, have no sexual contact for six months; abstinence will increase your spiritual magnetism.

"When, at the end of that time, you come together physically, think of that person. Think also of God. If you follow my advice in all these respects, that soul will be born to you."

They were faithful to what I'd told them, and, some time later, that very soul was drawn to be born in their family.

CONCEPTION

The soul enters the body at the moment of conception. When the sperm and ovum unite, there is a flash of light in the astral world. Souls there that are ready to be reborn, if their vibration matches that of the flash of light, rush to get in. Sometimes two or more get in at the same time, and the woman has twins, triplets, or even—well!

It is important, therefore, to come together physically with an uplifted consciousness. That flash generated in the astral world reflects the couple's state of consciousness, especially as it was during the moment of physical union.

Parents and Children

LOVE OF PARENTS AND CHILDREN

God is perfect love. Mankind, patterned after Him, is a reflection of His love. Human beings were propelled out of God, but even those children who are matter-truant children are kept ever tied to Him by long, invisible strings of His love, by which He gradually pulls them back to their home in Him. When man is selfish and wicked, he tries to pull away from God. When he loves truly and purely, he automatically, supported by subconscious will, follows that invisible thread of love which pulls him back toward God. Though God sent His mortal children far from Him, still He kept the gates of love open, that they may return at last to His home of perfection.

God foresaw that, blessed with the divine gift of free will, His children would misuse their freedom. He therefore insisted on becoming toward them the wise father to protect those children who were helpless or erring. Not satisfied with fatherly reason, He became also the mother, whose unconditional love for her erring children might help them to return home through the avenue of purely giving love. God became also, for parents, their loving children, to purify their conjugal love and expand it beyond the boundaries of inwardly turned selfishness. Divine love expands when it flows outward from two united hearts into a third heart of the child.

This does not mean, of course, that everyone has to marry in order to perfect his love from human to divine love. Human love can be transformed into divine love in a superior way by "marrying" the soul to the Spirit in the temple of meditation. The soul loves to meditate, for in meditation lies its greatest joy: contact with the loving Spirit. All persons who meditate devoutly succeed at last in manifesting pure, divine love.

The Relationship Between Parents and Children

The relationship between parents and children is a metaphysical and inexorable law of God, who is love; He brought us into these bodies through the love of two people. By love alone, therefore, can we find our way back to God. Parental and filial love is the laboratory in which human love can be transformed into perfect love. God manifests through conjugal love, and that love then becomes purified through sacrificing, expanding love for the child.

If parents and children will remember that their relationship is not accidental, but is due to a divine plan, then they, by their mutual kindness, will expand the love in their hearts during this earthly training. Mutual regard is the altar through which God's love becomes manifested.

Parents and children should be careful not to express undue familiarity. They should base their relationship also, not on force or authority, but on love. If they fill their hearts with unkindness, they can never learn to love God, who is love. True, unselfish love is developed at the altar of parental and filial love. The echo of God's love is silenced when harsh speech, unkindness, selfishness, or distrust vibrate through the body temple.

Responsibility of Parents and Children

Parents should look upon their every child as an honored temple, where their conjugal love can be purified and expanded, to become reflected, in time, in filial love. They should feel that they are serving God in those little temples. The children, too, should look upon their parents as visible representatives of God on earth.

Parents should never scold their children before others. If they are harsh or unkind to them, owing to lack of self-control or to bad habits in themselves, they will surely prevent God from expanding His love from those parental hearts to the hearts of their children. Parents should take care not, by continuous harshness, to bring their children to rebellion or resentment. They should give strong, loving suggestions to their erring children. They should also give them only necessities, not luxuries. Do not enslave your children to material things or to selfish greed. Well-to-do parents should be careful not to spoil their children with too much money and possessions.

It is important never to be too seriously attached to anything or anyone. A mother should train herself to say, "My child, when he grows up and moves away, or even if he dies, is taken away from me that God may glorify him. I am happy for his sake." When the mother can withdraw her natural human attachment, she will understand what true love is. Attachment cannot foster that love. Rather, it destroys love, and is, indeed, the source of much misery. One can be plunged into just as much misery in the loss of a hut as in the loss of a palace.

Children should be able to look upon their parents as channels through which God's love is first awakened in them. Children who disobey or dishonor their parents are rebels against that flow of divine love. If you, as a child, are scolded thoughtlessly before others by your parents, take care never to be disrespectful or resentful toward them. When either parents or children torment one another, they persecute the indwelling, ever gentle, Almighty God.

The Importance of Environment to a Child

The outward environment of one's early life is especially important in stimulating or stifling the child's inner, instinctive environment. One is born with a prenatal mental environment, which can be stimulated and reinforced in its influence if one's outer environment supports that inner environment. If, however, the outer environment is different from the inner environment, that inner influence is likely to be suppressed. An instinctively bad child may thus, by suppression of his naturally bad inclinations, be transformed by good company. The opposite also can happen: an instinctively good child may have that goodness suppressed. On the other hand, if he is placed in good company, his goodness will increase. Your outer environment, conjoined with your inner environment, through past as well as through recently acquired habits, controls your present life and molds your tastes and habits of this life.

Children may have either very good or very bad tendencies. Again, they may have only somewhat good or somewhat bad tendencies. Very few children are born with their good and evil exactly balanced. Always there is a little less bad in them than good, or vice versa. It is a Law of Nature that, if you are a little less bad than good, the evil in you will be transformed by the greater power of good. If, on the other hand, you have a little less good than bad, your goodness will gradually become absorbed by the greater number and strength of your evil tendencies.

Through reaction to your outer environment from early childhood on, you create your inner mental environment in this life. This inner environment—your thoughts and mental habits—almost automatically guides your actions. If a boy lives where people abhor drink, he forms a dislike of alcohol. If, then, he then goes to live among people who are alcoholics, he will be more likely to remain uninfluenced by them.

Whatever qualities you have now, make it a point to remain ever awake and aware, in thought, will, perception, and intuition, of the effects of every act. Be like a good photographer, always ready to take mental pictures of exemplary conduct, and to pass over examples of bad behavior. Your highest happiness will lie in being ever willing to learn from experience, and to behave accordingly.

My Experience with Will Power as a Child

When a baby cries, it is usually because it feels some physical need. The first expression of will, arising from that bodily condition, is called "physiological will."

As the baby grows, and is directed by its mother's will, it expresses "mechanical" or "unthinking will," for its will is guided by the mother.

I shall tell you of an experience I had when I was a baby. I remember being in that state of mechanical will, always doing just as mother told me. Everyone called me an angel. One day I was taken to a drugstore, where I saw some little orange-colored candies. I felt very much attracted to those candies, and asked my nurse to buy some for me. He refused and, instead, took me home; I said nothing about it.

I had my dinner. Afterward, I told my mother I wanted some candy. She said: "No, go to bed." A little later I said: "Mother, I want those little, orange-colored candies."

"Go to bed," Mother said. Thereupon I cried all the more loudly: "I want those orange-colored candies!" I continued in my determination to have my way, unheeding of her appeal to forget about them. Mother finally had to go out and actually wake up the drugstore owner to obtain those candies for me.

I was happy. Why so? Because I had suddenly exercised my *own* will power. I found it the most wonderful feeling.

The next morning, of course, I was called a "naughty baby." But it was only because I had had my own way.

Parents, don't break your child's will by always denying him his inconvenient requests, just because he is a baby. When I made up my mind that I wanted something that I knew could do me no harm, the members of my family had to consent. I always listened to reason, and if ever I was wrong I was willing to be corrected. When I was right, however, even if the whole family united against me, I remained firm.

Remember, when your young children seem self-willed about something that isn't wrong, and may even be righteous, don't call them naughty. Don't curtail their freedom. Listen to their little desires, and offer suggestions based on love and understanding. Reason with them. If they insist, don't say anything. Let them have their own little hard knocks, if necessary. In that way, they'll come to understand. And they'll learn much sooner what is right.

Parents often impose their wills on their children. That is why as a child, I never liked to pray. My problem was, I didn't understand, for myself, the purpose of prayer. But when I understood that it was not a matter of propitiating an unwilling God, but of offering love to Him from my soul, I was able to pray sincerely, and everyone in my home listened. Give freedom to your young child and suggest to him only with love what you think is right. Remember, it's important that the will power of your children be developed.

Try not to ask anything of your child that you can't back with a good reason.

"HONOR THY FATHER AND MOTHER"

While everyone should honor his father and mother, he should not be so attached to them that if they ask him to leave the path of renunciation or meditation on God, he should obey them and forsake God. God should come first in one's life, before every other person or desire. One's engagement with God in meditation must be considered above everything else. Indeed, no one can keep any other engagement in life without the borrowed energy and mental and muscular strength he derives from God.

Chapter 5

SEPARATION AND LOSS

THE VEIL OF SUPERFICIAL ATTRACTION

I remember a couple who came to me in Phoenix and asked me to marry them "immediately." I told them, "I must know the people I marry. I want to meditate on your request. Please come back tomorrow." At this proposed delay, the man was furious.

When they returned the next day, he pressed me, "Is it all right?"

"No," I said.

He was enraged once more. "Let's get out of here, dear! We can get married by someone else."

They had almost reached the door when I called to them. "Remember my words: You will never be happy together. You will find that out when it is too late. But please, I urge you, at least don't kill each other!"

They were married elsewhere. Soon afterward they came to Mt. Washington just to show me how happy they were. I said nothing, but inside me I thought, "You don't know what a boiling cauldron is hidden under that lid!"

Six months later they returned. This time they knelt humbly before me and confessed, "We didn't realize how different our natures were. If you hadn't warned us, we would surely have ended up killing each other." Under the influence of emotional intoxication, you see, they hadn't observed the explosive violence inherent in their natures, and therefore in their relationship.

People must learn to look behind the veil of superficial attraction. Without soul harmony there can be no true love.

ATTACHMENT AND LOVE

Attachment is a sort of blind feeling that causes torture to the soul. It does not accomplish anything. Attachment is not love. Real love is happy only in the happiness of the beloved. You say that you love your wonderful friend, you enjoy his company, you love to serve him. Then he leaves you. If, after he has gone, you forget him, you are heartless. If, day and night, you make yourself miserable thinking of your loss, you are foolish. That attachment will do neither you nor your friend any good. Rather, you should say that some day you will understand why he left. Wish him happiness, and pray that, since he has gone, it is for his own betterment. Whatever is God's will, and whatever is best for him, that should be your wish.

DIFFICULT MARRIAGES AND DIVORCE

If you are already married, but mis-mated, try if possible to make the best of the situation. If, for the sake of the children, if you have them, or for some other good reason, you want to remain with your spouse, try to overcome your own mental shortcomings, and let understanding triumph. If you can manage that, you will have learned an important lesson in the art of right behavior, and in the magnetic way of getting along with everybody.

A man who can conquer a nagging wife by diplomacy, without becoming "hen-pecked," can win anyone to his side. A woman who can conquer an unfaithful husband by forgiving, continuous, silent love and by a continuous demonstration of kindness and unshakability, can remain always in the impregnable castle of inner happiness.

If you love your husband, try to forgive all his faults, even that of unfaithfulness, and give him sufficient time to recover from his inner weakness by the balm of your continuous love. Most wives add the chili sauce of burning words and unkindness to the erring husband, even when he is inwardly penitent. That results in open rebellion. Do not bring your misunderstanding to the point of poisonous outbursts. Mentally hint, by your increased loving, that you want your husband to be healed. When a man is wrong, and he knows that he is wrong, he hates to be told of his error. Not wanting to be labeled, he rebels.

If you want to get along peaceably with your mate, first refrain from using harsh speech. If you want your mate to stop using harsh language, refrain from using it yourself, first. Harsh words bring forth increasing volleys of harsh words. They never stop those volleys. Why go to the extremes of making the one you live with hate you inwardly? For, consider the results: flying rolling pins, black eyes, and in the end, divorce. Silently correct your own faults and remove any cause that may have given rise to harsh words, quarrels, and hatred between you and your mate.

If you want the Heavenly Father to show you the way to marital harmony, make up your mind to be kind in thought, word, and deed to your mate, even if, in the end, you both decide to separate. Above all, make up your mind not to be ugly or hateful or rough in speech merely because your partner is like that. If you hate ugliness in your partner, do not allow that same mental squalor to soil your own lips, actions, or thoughts. If the two of you end up having to part, do so with kindness. That way, perhaps your mate will inwardly acknowledge his or her faults, and repent inwardly. If, on the other hand, you have to live together, don't add to your partner's annoyance by increasing his or her misunderstandings. Seal your lips. Avoid unkindness in thought, speech, and action. Win your mate by offering continuous kindness, and by courtesy in every action.

If you must part, you might write a love letter like the following: "Very dear one, we once loved each other. Let us again remember that love. Since we entered into a marriage partnership in good will, meaning well, and since we failed to make our marriage a success, let us part in kindness and in the memory of our old love. I am leaving you in order to preserve my kind thoughts of you forever, for I shall ever hold our past love as very sacred in the vault of my memory."

After deep meditation, remain for a long time with the joy of the Father. Then concentrate at the point between the eyebrows, and mentally repeat before going to bed, or upon waking: "Father, we came together. Teach us to live together in love, or, if it is Thy will, teach us to part in love and mutual understanding."

WHY OUR LOVED ONES DIE

God was not satisfied with creating only fruits and flowers and scenic beauties for man's entertainment. He also took the form, personally, of parents to give protection to the baby-man. Not satisfied with only protecting children through the compelling instinct of parental love, God also took the form of friends in order to extend to him unlimited love. Thus, God's love plays hide-and-seek in the human heart.

The baby grows up loving its parents. He grows to adulthood. His parents then die, and he feels a pang for that lost love. He seeks solace by falling in love, and finds a powerful conjugal love swaying his heart, eclipsing all other forms of love.

As time goes on, he loses the first ardor of his conjugal love. He wonders, "Whither has my overwhelming love fled?"

Aged couples develop friendly understanding for each other, but they never again can love each other with the passionate love of their youth. Love hides behind the screen of material attachments, and nearly always remains hidden there forever, never coming out to display its heart-dissolving form.

When your parents die, and you lose their love, and when you grow old and can no longer feel the ardor of conjugal love, remember this: love itself is not lost.

Real love still hides in the breast of every living being—even in the flowers and the silent stars. God conceals His love there that you may find it again, beholding it decorated with the robes of eternal splendor.

Why does Nature make us love some people so dearly, then only to snatch them away from us—at least, from our view?

Divine Love plays hide-and-seek with us in life, then hides behind the veil of death, that we may seek it still and find it in the secret bower of Omnipresence. Love leads us through the endless mazes of life and death in order to lead us to the land where Perfect Love shines in full brilliancy. Indeed, even in death, love lives on.

The moon laughs at lovers who have sworn eternal love to one another, for their skulls are now strewn over the earth, and none can speak that human love any longer.

Yet, *true* Love says, "Let the moon and destiny laugh at human inconstancy and impermanence, but they can never laugh at Me. It is I who broke these prisons of bones and flesh, in which mortal man wanted to keep Me caged forever. Behold, however: Although I have broken up their human loves, I have yet drawn their souls to follow the trail of heartfelt pangs to My hiding place at the heart of all space. Here, at last, true lovers will rest forever in My unending, ever-new bliss. It is My undying love alone they sought through other, much lesser loves."

Divine Love says to all, "If you love Me, you will love Me not in one being, but in all. Remember, though you try to cage Me in one person, I will destroy in the end the body-frame which holds him. I do so that you may learn to find Me in all."

Chapter 6

THE FRIEND OF ALL FRIENDS

O Father, when I was blind I found not a door which led to Thee, but now that Thou hast opened my eyes, I find doors everywhere: through the hearts of flowers, through the voice of friendship, through sweet memories of all lovely experiences. Every gust of my prayer opens an unentered door in the vast temple of Thy presence.

With the love of all human loves, I have come to love Thee, Thou God of all loves. Thou art the protecting father. Thou art the little child, lisping love to his parents. Thou art the mother, showering infinite kindnesses. Thou dost flow in the all-surrendering love of the lover to the beloved. Thou art the love of friends. Purify me with the reverence of a servant to his master. Teach me to love Thee with all pure love, for Thou art the fountain of love, heavenly and earthly. Bathe me in the spray of all loves.

BUDDHA AND THE COURTESAN

Buddha and his disciples underwent a curious incident which left the disciples, for a time, puzzled as to the character of their Master. The Buddha and his disciples were all vowed to celibacy and the renunciation of carnal love. And yet, one day, when the great Buddha and his disciples were resting in the cool shade of a tree, a courtesan approached him, attracted by the glowing body and face of the Master. No sooner had she seen the celestial face of the Lord Buddha than she fell in love with him, and with open arms ran to Buddha to embrace and kiss him, exclaiming loudly: "O beautiful Shining One, I love thee."

The celibate disciples were astonished to hear the Buddha's reply to the courtesan. He said, "Beloved, I love thee too. Do not touch me now, however. Not yet."

The courtesan replied: "You call me beloved and to me you are my beloved. Why, then, do you object to my touching you?"

The great Buddha replied: "Beloved, again I tell thee, I will touch thee later; not now. Then I will prove my true love for thee." The disciples were shocked, thinking that the Master had fallen in love with this courtesan.

Years later, as Buddha was meditating with his disciples, he suddenly cried out: "I must go! My beloved, the courtesan, is calling me; she needs me now. I must fulfill my promise to her." The disciples ran after their Master, hoping somehow to save him, though he seemed madly in love with the courtesan.

The great Buddha, followed anxiously by his worried disciples, came to the same tree where they had met the courtesan before. There she lay, with her beautiful body covered with putrefying, odorous smallpox sores. The disciples cringed and held themselves far from her. The Buddha, however, took her decaying body, held it like a child, and placed her head on his lap, whispering to her: "Beloved, I have come to prove my love to thee, and to fulfill my promise to touch thee. I have waited a long time to demonstrate my true love, for I love thee when everyone else has ceased loving thee. I touch thee when all thy summer friends fear to touch thee any more." Thus speaking, Buddha healed the courtesan and invited her, now purged by him of all carnal desire, to join his growing band of disciples.

Personal love is selfish, and considers its own comforts—often at the cost of everything else. Divine love is unselfish; it seeks the happiness of the object of its love, and is not limited or partial. God loves both the wicked and the good equally, for they are His children. All those who aspire to know Him must prove to Him that their love, like His love, is for all. When a soul proves to the Heavenly Father that he loves his good and evil brothers equally, then the Father will say: "My noble son, I accept thy love, for thou lovest all with My love, even as I do." To love those who love you is natural, but ego-inspired. To love those who do not love you, or who even hate you, is to express supernatural love, to see God in all.

WHAT IS REAL LOVE?

Reflect always on this deep truth: You belong to no one, and no one belongs to you. You are on this earth for only a little while. Your real reason for being here is altogether different from anything you may have imagined.

Your family claims you as its own. Should you die, however, and be reborn next door, will they love you? Will they even recognize you?

Your friends claim you as theirs, but if you cease in some way to please them, perhaps even by some trivial misunderstanding, how many of them will remain loyal to you? Not all of them, by any means.

People say that they love others, but in fact they love themselves. For the love they feel for others is to the extent only that others please *them*.

Real love finds happiness, even at the cost of great personal sacrifice, in the happiness of the one loved. How many people love in that way? Very few! And of those few, how many find their love reciprocated? Fewer still!

Only our love for God is ever fully requited—indeed, far more than requited. For God understands us when all others misunderstand. God loves us when others turn against us. God remembers us when everyone forgets us. We are God's, and God's alone, for all eternity.

PURE LOVE

The sun and moon and earth and all things are held together by the bonding force of God's love. If we want to know Him, we must not keep our love isolated and small, but conjoin it to divine love. Through all the dance of life and death, know that God is love. The only purpose of life should be to find that love. There is no greater tonic. It can beautify man in both body and mind. Love cannot be described or defined: It can only be experienced, as a deep feeling.

All love, in its native purity, is God's love. If pure love shines in your soul, you will be clothed with God's ever-attracting, universal beauty and infinite love. All nations should come together in the temple of universal love and understanding. Love alone will last. The laws of God are the laws of brotherhood and love.

Although man's love is born in his human relations and in recognition of mutual usefulness, yet pure love, as it evolves spiritually, transcends all outer relationships and becomes freed from every condition of mutual usefulness. Although love is born in that sense of usefulness, one ceases to be aware of any such outward condition. A mother's love for her child may be taken as an example, for it is unconditional. A mother may love even a wicked child.

Expand Our Love

Our love must not be limited to those who are near to us. The divine purpose of close relationships is to expand that love. Nature breaks the ties of family life only to teach us that the love we give our family needs to be extended also to our neighbors, our friends, our country, and to all nations. One who does not love his family cannot love his neighbor or his country. One who does not first love his country cannot learn to love all countries.

Love is a condition of the mind and heart which essentially transcends all relationships. We should worship God above all through all these relationships. God can be loved as Father, Mother, Master, Friend, or the Divine Beloved of all hearts.

Love must never remain circumscribed in littleness. Through the gates of friendship, conjugal affection, parental love, and the love of one's fellow beings and of all animate creatures, we can enter into the kingdom of Divine Love. Pure love does not come by talking, but by culturing it gradually in the soil of an ever-increasing, ever-expanding feeling of sympathy and friendship toward all existence.

That person who has never loved anyone in particular can never love all humanity. One who has never loved his fellow beings, and even birds and animals, can never love God. Only in the soil of the heart where human love grows can divine love grow.

EXTENDING THE KINGDOM OF YOUR HEART

To feel God, you must extend the territory of heart-felt feeling itself. You feel, at present, only with your own heart. Try every day to feel more and more also with the hearts of others. Feel their woes, their struggles, their joys, their fulfillments. To feel the hearts of others means that you must remain not only absorbed in feeling for yourself, but to work and also spend for others as for yourself, to love and protect them with the same interest and enthusiasm as you feel for yourself.

Begin with sensitivity to the needs of one person. Day by day, widen that circle of sensitivity to include more individuals. Let your feelings for them be active, not merely passive and sentimental. Try to love others *actively* by helping them every day, especially those who love you. Keep on acting in this spirit until you find yourself able to do so even with respect to those who care nothing for you. At last, let the feeling of love, good will, and spontaneous helpfulness go forth to enfold those who don't know you, and even those who hate you. This is a real, practical way by which the soul can expand its victories from heart to heart, ever enlarging its boundaries until at last it recovers its rightful kingdom of Divine Consciousness in the hearts of all creatures.

Feel the One Heart of God

Your unceasing love and unselfish readiness to help others without distinction of sex, caste, or creed will make your heart's feelings broad enough to accommodate all humanity. Once the love of all human beings and, indeed, of all things living is included in your heart's feelings, your heart will merge with and become one with the Heart of God. Feeling all hearts as one, you will feel the Cosmic Heart beating behind all hearts. Going beyond the limitations of individual, selfish love, and feeling rather the same love for all, you will feel the One Great Love which burns everlastingly and forever as a pure white flame on the universal altar of all hearts. Speak to your own soul silently: "I shall drink Thy Love alone from all cups, O God! From the gold, silver, and crystal cups of the world, and from the shining, invisible cups of human hearts, I will drink Thy Love alone!"

Recognizing the God-love burning secretly in all heart lamps, you will become aware of God's love alone, flowing through everybody and everything.

Every time you meet a receptive human being, show him your interest in his physical, mental, and spiritual welfare. *Never neglect to do whatever you can for yourself in the forms of others.* To know the Spirit, you must become the Spirit, finding yourself manifested through the bodies and minds of all. Make the bubble of ego one with the ocean of Spirit. Make it vast, so vast that you behold all the bubbles of living beings floating there. Break the boundaries of small selfishness, and include in boundless ego-selflessness all living beings.

Chant the song of cosmic consciousness:

"So be Thou, my Lord,
Thou and I, never apart;
Wave of the sea,
Dissolve in the Sea!
I am the bubble;
Make me the Sea!"

Break the walls of selfishness. Make your love vast and deep enough to contain all beings.

Love God through All Hearts

Drink the nectar of divine love in all hearts. See every heart as your own wine cup from which you drink the fresh ambrosia of God's love. Drink not this Love from one heart only, but drink it freely from all hearts: the love of God alone.

Feel God as divine love, potentially manifested in all hearts. Feel God in the impartial love you feel for all humanity, and in the tender love you feel for all created beings.

And then you will be able to pray the only prayer I ever pray for myself: "Heavenly Father, may Thy love shine forever on the sanctuary of my devotion. And may my devotion for Thee forever burn on the altar of my memory. May I be able to kindle love for Thee on all altar-hearts."

EXPANDING LOVE

I will behold God Himself bestowing His divine love on me through the love of all those who love me.

All desire for love I will purify and satisfy in the sacred divine love of God.

All earthly friends, who today seem so real, will some day become unreal, as they pass away. Then, your only true, lasting friend will prove to be the One whose love now seems intangible. Cry for God in the depths of night, steadfastly, deeply, determinedly. Do not stop until He comes to you.

O Divine Mother, teach me to use the gift of Thy love in my heart to love the members of my family more than myself. Bless me, that I may love my neighbors more than my family. Expand me, so that I love my country more than my neighbors, and that I love my world and all human brethren more than my country, neighbors, family, and myself.

Lastly, teach me to love Thee more than anything else, for it is Thy love with which I love everything. Without Thee I cannot love anybody or anything.

Father Divine, teach me to enter through the portals of family love, and through the love of my friends, into the mansion of wider social love. Teach me, then, to pass through the doors of social love into the wider mansion of international love. Teach me to pass through the portals of international love into the endless territory of divine love, in which I may perceive all objects, both animate and inanimate, as breathing and living by Thy love.

Teach me to tarry not at any of the fascinating but lesser shrines of family, social or international love. Teach me to pass beyond those minor gods, confined as their dominion is to small territories of selfish, human love, until, passing through the last gate of selfless love, I enter into the endless territory of divine love, where I shall find all living, semi-living, or sleeping things to be my own.

INDEX

adultery, 90
affection, 26
Americans, 17, 57
anger, 33
apology, 52
attachment, love and, 114–15
Autobiography of a Yogi
    (Yogananda), 9

Babaji, 73
beauty, 38
    infatuation of, 65
    physical, 53, 65
    standard of, 53
blind hate, 16
"Buddha and Courtesan"
    story, 126–28

celibacy, 96
Chariot of life, 25
children
    environment's importance
        to, 103–5
    of God, 57
    love for, 22
    love of, 99–105

children continued
    mothers' love for, 130
    relationship with parents,
        100–101
    responsibility of, 101–3
    teaching, 88
    tendencies of, 104
    will power of, 105–7
Christ consciousness, 55–56, 57
compulsion, 22
conception, 98
consciousness, 46
    divine, 133
    of equality, 22
    inner, 41
    See also Christ
        consciousness;
        Cosmic consciousness
Cosmic consciousness, 46, 58
    attaining, 20
    song of, 134
Cosmic heart, 46
Cosmic soul, 17, 58
courtesy, 26
Creative force
    regulating, 92–94
    spiritualizing and
        transmuting, 88–97

criticism
constructive, 36
correct, 36
destructive, 36–37
divine, 37
internal, 36
kind, 39

death
love and, 119
of loved ones, 118–20
of parents, 119
desire, 67
devotees, 67–68
Divine friendship, 15, 17, 24, 54
Divine law, 33
Divine potential, 9
Divine soul, 20
Divine teacher, 17
divorce, 69, 115–18

East West, 10
ego, 20, 56
elderly couples, 90, 119
enemies, 19
converting to friends, 51–55

enemies continued
friends to, 22–23
God in, 23
hatred of, 34
love for, 18–19
as neighbors, 50
environment
children and, 103–5
inner mental, 47, 104
role of, 46–47
secret to happy, 47–48

familiarity, 16
family
love, 17, 20, 58
world, 50–51
faults, 31–32, 37
flattery
love of, 39–40
truth *vs.,* 39–40
forgiveness, 19
low light of, 34
for others, 37
Francis, Saint, 72
free will, 99
friends
converting enemies to, 51–55

friends continued
    cosmic, 15
    divine, 54
    to enemies, 22–23
    gaining, 15–19
    in past incarnations, 52–55
    See also Great Friend
friendship
    call of, 57–59
    of God, 15, 19, 23, 58
    heart of, 19
    as hybrid of souls, 26
    instinct, 27
    laws of, 16–18
    love as God's, 15
    pure, 23
    service as keynote of, 45–46
    true, 21–23
    wisdom in, 21
    See also Divine friendship

God
    as bridegroom, 72–73
    children of, 57
    in enemies, 23
    feeling One heart of, 133–35
    friendship of, 15, 19, 23, 58

God continued
    love of, 15, 18, 21, 125
    loving through all hearts, 135
Great Friend, 16
Great Source, 41

happiness, 48, 129
    love finding, 129
    soul, 67
harmony, 25
harsh words, 116–17
hatred, 23
    blind, 16
    of enemies, 34
health, 38
heart
    cosmic, 46
    extending kingdom of, 132–35
    feeling One of God, 133–35
    of friendship, 19
    loving God through all, 135
Hindus, 17
**"Honor Thy Father and
    Mother,"** 107–8
humility, 52
husbands
    behavior plan for, 75–78

husbands continued
    true ideals of, 69
    See also Life companion

idealism, 69–70
Infinity, 56
Inner Culture, 10
inner weakness, 31

jealousy, 37–39, 64
    constructive, 38–39
    curing disease of, 84–85
    destructive, 38–39
    in marriage, 81–84
    as self-love, 82, 85
Jesus, 16, 72
    sacrifice of, 50
    strength of, 18
Joy of Father, 117–18
judgment, 31–33

kindness, 32, 83
    See also Unkindness
Kingdom of heart, extending,
    132–35

language
    courteous, 34
    harsh words, 116–17
    sweet speech, 65
laws
    of cause and effect, 32
    divine, 33
    of friendship, 16–18
    ideal of marriage, 74–80
    of vibration, 22
life companion
    avoiding selection mistakes,
        73–74
    selecting, 63–68
"Lost Ear" story, 31
love
    attachment and, 114–15
    bathing in spray of all, 125
    for children, 22
    of children, 99–105
    conjugal, 84, 101
    death and, 119
    divine, 16, 20, 71, 120, 127–
        28, 131–32, 137
    for enemies, 18–19
    expanding to all, 55–56,
        131–32, 136–37
    family, 17, 20, 58

finding happiness, 129
of flattery, 39–40
fountain of, 41
of God, 15, 18, 21, 125
human, 16
meditation on expanding, 59
mothers' for children, 130
of parents, 22, 99–105
personal, 127
pure, 129–32
real, 128–29
selfless, 56–59
for sense pleasures, 67–68
soul, 70
among souls, 15
supernatural, 128
unconditional, 65
See also Self-love
love letter, 117
loyalty, 92

magnetism
power of, 71–72
spiritual, 72
marriage
creating lasting, 68–74
difficulties in, 80–85, 115–18
high purpose of, 85–88

ideal laws of, 74–80
jealousy in, 81–84
for money/social position, 65
selecting life companion,
63–68
spiritual, 87
under stress of emotion, 66–67
when unnecessary, 74–75
married people, hints to, 95–97
meditation, 9, 82
on expanding love, 59
higher forms of, 86–87
temple of, 100
mental dirt, 31
mental unity, 64
moderation, 96
morals, 69
mothers, 130

nationality, Spirit as, 17, 58

Omnipresence, 17, 41
as country, 58
secret bower of, 119
social way to, 20–21
One
heart of God, 133–35
Spirit as, 24

over-sensitivity, 34–35

parents
    death of, 119
    love of, 22, 99–105
    relationship with children,
        100–101
    responsibility of, 101–3
pleasure, 48–49
    sense-pleasures, 67–68
    solace in true, 25
publicity
    of inner faults, 31–32
    thrill of, 66–67
purity
    of friendship, 23
    of love, 129–32
    souls dressed in, 65

reason, 68
relationships
    children/parents, 100–101
    purpose of, 131
relatives, 55

salvation, 19
sarcasm, 45
Satan
    inducements of, 82
    over-sensitivity and, 35
self-control, 67, 74–75
    methods for, 93–94
self-discipline, 96
selfishness, 53
    evil, 48–51
    example of, 49
    good, 48–51
selflessness, 25
self-love, 82, 85
self-pity, 35
self-preservation, 49
sense-pleasures, 67–68
sensitiveness, 34–35
service, as friendship keynote,
        45–46
sex. *See* Creative force
Shankara, 73
sociability, 57
soul(s), 17
    awakening, 9
    cosmic, 17, 58
    divine, 20
    dressed in purity, 65

soul(s) continued
  flowers of, 27
  friendship as hybrid of, 26
  happiness, 67
  kindred, 70
  love, 70
  love among, 15
  uniting, 21
Spirit, 46
  flame of, 16
  knowing, 134
  manifestation of, 51
  as nationality, 17, 58
  as One, 24
  unity of, 58
spiritual awakening, 9
spiritual child
  creating, 93
  drawing, 97
"Spiritual Critic" story, 40
spiritual development, 57, 58
subconscious, 68
superficial attraction, veil of, 113–14
sweet speech, 65

temptation, 68

true feelings, 26
true Self, 51
truth
  governing all life, 33
  flattery *vs.*, 39–40

ugliness of disposition, 53
unity
  mental, 64
  seeking complete, 70–71
  of Spirit, 58
unkindness, 33–34
unmarried people, hints to, 95–97
usefulness, 22

Whispers from Eternity
  (Yogananda), 10
wisdom, 65
  building of, 22
  in friendship, 21
wives
  adoring, young, 65
  behavior plan for, 78–80
  true ideals of, 69
  See also Life companion

world family, 50–51

Yoga, 9
Yogananda, Paramhansa, 9–10

List of Illustrations

1. Yogananda with Rajarshi just after Rajarshi's initiation into monkhood 13

2. Paramhansa Yogananda 29

3. Luther Burbank, beloved friend, with Yogananda. . . 43

4. Yogananda with sisters, Roma and Nalini. 61

5. "The Last Smile," Yogananda at the Biltmore Hotel, shortly before entering mahasamadhi 111

6. Yogananda with his guru, Swami Sri Yukteswar, in India, 1935 123

7. Yogananda with a small bear in Yellowstone National Park 139

About the Author

PARAMHANSA YOGANANDA

"As a bright light shining in the midst of darkness, so was Yogananda's presence in this world. Such a great soul comes on earth only rarely, when there is a real need among men."

—The Shankaracharya of Kanchipuram

Born in India in 1893, Paramhansa Yogananda was trained from his early years to bring India's ancient science of Self-realization to the West. In 1920 he moved to the United States to begin what was to develop into a worldwide work touching millions of lives. Americans were hungry for India's spiritual teachings, and for the liberating techniques of yoga.

In 1946 he published what has become a spiritual classic and one of the best-loved books of the twentieth century, *Autobiography of a Yogi*. In addition, Yogananda established headquarters for a worldwide work, wrote a number of books and study courses, gave lectures to thousands in most major cities across the United States, wrote music and poetry, and trained disciples. He was invited to the White House by Calvin Coolidge, and he initiated Mahatma Gandhi into Kriya Yoga, his most advanced meditation technique.

Yogananda's message to the West highlighted the unity of all religions, and the importance of love for God combined with scientific techniques of meditation.

Dear Reader,

Ananda is a worldwide work based on the same teachings expressed in this book—those of the great spiritual teacher, Paramhansa Yogananda. If you enjoyed this title, Crystal Clarity Publishers invites you to continue to deepen your spiritual life through the many avenues of Ananda Worldwide—including meditation communities, centers, and groups; online virtual community and webinars; retreat centers offering classes and teacher training in yoga and meditation; and more.

For special offers and discounts for first-time visitors to Ananda, visit:
http://www.crystalclarity.com/welcome

Feel free to contact us. We are here to serve you.

Joy to you,

Crystal Clarity Publishers

ANANDA WORLDWIDE

Ananda, a worldwide organization founded by Swami Kriyananda, offers spiritual support and resources based on the teachings of Paramhansa Yogananda. There are Ananda spiritual communities in Nevada City, Sacramento, and Palo Alto, California; Seattle, Washington; Portland and Laurelwood, Oregon; as well as a retreat center and European community in Assisi, Italy, and a community near New Delhi, India. Ananda supports more than 140 meditation groups worldwide.

For more information about Ananda's work, our communities, or meditation groups near you, please call 530.478.7560 or visit www.ananda.org.

THE EXPANDING LIGHT RETREAT

The Expanding Light is the largest retreat center in the world to share exclusively the teachings of Paramhansa Yogananda. Situated in the Ananda Village community, it offers the opportunity to experience spiritual life in a contemporary ashram setting. The varied, year-round schedule of classes and programs on yoga, meditation, and spiritual practice includes Karma Yoga, Personal Retreat, Spiritual Travel, and online learning. The Ananda School of Yoga & Meditation offers certified yoga, yoga therapist, spiritual counselor, and meditation teacher trainings. Large groups are welcome.

The teaching staff are experts in Kriya Yoga meditation and all aspects of Yogananda's teachings. All staff members live at Ananda Village and bring an uplifting approach to their areas of service. The serene natural setting and delicious vegetarian meals help provide an ideal environment for a truly meaningful visit.

For more information, please call 800.346.5350
or visit www.expandinglight.org.

CRYSTAL CLARITY PUBLISHERS

Crystal Clarity Publishers offers many additional resources to assist you in your spiritual journey, including many other books (see the following pages for some of them), a wide variety of inspirational and relaxation music composed by Swami Kriyananda, and yoga and meditation videos. To request a catalog, place an order for the above products, or to find out more information, please contact us at:

Crystal Clarity Publishers / www.crystalclarity.com
14618 Tyler Foote Rd. / Nevada City, CA 95959
TOLL FREE: 800.424.1055 or 530.478.7600 / FAX: 530.478.7610
EMAIL: clarity@crystalclarity.com

For our online catalog, complete with secure ordering, please visit our website.

The original 1946 unedited edition of Yogananda's spiritual masterpiece

AUTOBIOGRAPHY OF A YOGI
Paramhansa Yogananda

Autobiography of a Yogi is one of the best-selling Eastern philosophy titles of all time, with millions of copies sold, named one of the best and most influential books of the twentieth century. This highly prized reprinting of the original 1946 edition is the only one available free from textual changes made after Yogananda's death. Yogananda was the first yoga master of India whose mission was to live and teach in the West.

In this updated edition are bonus materials, including a last chapter that Yogananda wrote in 1951, without posthumous changes. This new edition also includes the eulogy that Yogananda wrote for Gandhi, and a new foreword and afterword by Swami Kriyananda, one of Yogananda's close, direct disciples.

Also available in unabridged audiobook (MP3) format, read by Swami Kriyananda.

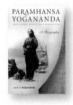

PARAMHANSA YOGANANDA
A Biography with Personal Reflections and Reminiscences
Swami Kriyananda

Paramhansa Yogananda's classic *Autobiography of a Yogi* is more about the saints Yogananda met than about himself—in spite of Yogananda's astonishing accomplishments.

Now, one of Yogananda's direct disciples relates the untold story of this great spiritual master and world teacher: his teenage miracles, his challenges in coming to America, his national lecture campaigns, his struggles to fulfill his world-changing mission amid incomprehension and painful betrayals, and his ultimate triumphant achievement. Kriyananda's subtle grasp of his guru's inner nature reveals Yogananda's many-sided greatness. Includes many never-before-published anecdotes.

Also available in unabridged audiobook (MP3) format, read by Swami Kriyananda.

THE NEW PATH
My Life with Paramhansa Yogananda
Swami Kriyananda

When Swami Kriyananda discovered *Autobiography of a Yogi* in 1948, he was totally new to Eastern teachings. This is a great advantage to the Western reader, since Kriyananda walks us along the yogic path as he discovers it from the moment of his initiation as a disciple of Yogananda. With winning honesty, humor, and deep insight, he shares his journey on the spiritual path through personal stories and experiences.

Through more than four hundred stories of life with Yogananda, we tune in more deeply to this great master and to the teachings he brought to the West. This book is an ideal complement to *Autobiography of a Yogi.*

Also available in unabridged audiobook (MP3) format, read by Swami Kriyananda.

THE ESSENCE OF THE BHAGAVAD GITA
Explained by Paramhansa Yogananda
As Remembered by his disciple, Swami Kriyananda

Rarely in a lifetime does a new spiritual classic appear that has the power to change people's lives and transform future generations. This is such a book.

This revelation of India's best-loved scripture approaches it from a fresh perspective, showing its deep allegorical meaning and its down-to-earth practicality. The themes presented are universal: how to achieve victory in life in union with the divine; how to prepare for life's "final exam," death, and what happens afterward; and how to triumph over all pain and suffering.

Also available in unabridged audiobook (MP3) format, read by Swami Kriyananda.

the original booklet later published as *The Law of Success*. In addition, you will learn how to find your purpose in life, develop habits of success and eradicate habits of failure, develop your will power and magnetism, and thrive in the right job.

Winner of the 2011 International Book Award for the Best Self-Help Book of the Year

HOW TO HAVE COURAGE, CALMNESS AND CONFIDENCE
The Wisdom of Yogananda Series, Volume 5
Paramhansa Yogananda

Everyone can be courageous, calm, and confident, because these are qualities of the soul. Hypnotized with material thinking and desires, many of us have lost touch with our inner power. In this potent book of spiritual wisdom, Paramhansa Yogananda shares the most effective steps for reconnecting with your divine nature.

HOW TO ACHIEVE GLOWING HEALTH AND VITALITY
The Wisdom of Yogananda Series, VOLUME 6
Paramhansa Yogananda

Paramhansa Yogananda, a foremost spiritual teacher of modern times, offers practical, wide-ranging, and fascinating suggestions on how to have more energy and live a radiantly healthy life. The principles in this book promote physical health and all-round well-being, mental clarity, and ease and inspiration in your spiritual life.

Readers will discover the priceless Energization Exercises for rejuvenating the body and mind, the fine art of conscious relaxation, and helpful diet tips for health and beauty.

HOW TO AWAKEN YOUR TRUE POTENTIAL
The Wisdom of Yogananda Series, VOLUME 7
Paramhansa Yogananda

Every soul is on a journey of self-discovery. The length of the journey depends on the choices we make. We can cooperate with the flow of God's positive influence within us—or we can resist and cling to our familiar limitations and habits—the choice is ours.

Additional Titles from Crystal Clarity

Demystifying Patanjali
The Wisdom of Paramhansa Yogananda Presented by his direct disciple, Swami Kriyananda

The Essence of Self-Realization
The Wisdom of Paramhansa Yogananda Recorded, Compiled, and Edited by his disciple, Swami Kriyananda

Conversations with Yogananda
Recorded, with Reflections, by his disciple, Swami Kriyananda

Revelations of Christ
Proclaimed by Paramhansa Yogananda Presented by his disciple, Swami Kriyananda

Whispers from Eternity
Paramhansa Yogananda Edited by his disciple, Swami Kriyananda

The Rubaiyat of Omar Khayyam
Paramhansa Yogananda Edited by his disciple, Swami Kriyananda

Meditation for Starters with CD
Swami Kriyananda

Intuition for Starters
Swami Kriyananda

Chakras for Starters
Savitri Simpson

Vegetarian Cooking for Starters
Diksha McCord

The Art and Science of Raja Yoga
Swami Kriyananda

Awaken to Superconsciousness
Swami Kriyananda

Living Wisely, Living Well
Swami Kriyananda

The Bhagavad Gita
According to Paramhansa Yogananda
Edited by his disciple,
Swami Kriyananda

How to Meditate
Jyotish Novak

Self-Expansion Through Marriage
Swami Kriyananda

The Time Tunnel
Swami Kriyananda

God Is for Everyone
Inspired by Paramhansa Yogananda
As taught to and understood by
his disciple, Swami Kriyananda

Religion in the New Age
Swami Kriyananda

The Art of Supportive Leadership
J. Donald Walters (Swami
Kriyananda)

Money Magnetism
J. Donald Walters (Swami
Kriyananda)

Two Souls: Four Lives
Catherine Kairavi

In Divine Friendship
Swami Kriyananda

30-Day Essentials for Marriage
Jyotish Novak

30-Day Essentials for Career
Jyotish Novak

Education for Life
J. Donald Walters (Swami
Kriyananda)

The Peace Treaty
J. Donald Walters (Swami
Kriyananda)

Pilgrimage to Guadalupe
Swami Kriyananda

Love Perfected, Life Divine
Swami Kriyananda

Walking With William of Normandy
A Paramhansa Yogananda Pilgrimage Guide
Richard Salva

The Yoga of Ghost Hunting
Richard Salva

The Reincarnation of Abraham Lincoln
Richard Salva

The Yoga of Abraham Lincoln
Richard Salva

Lessons in Meditation
Jyotish Novak

A Handbook on Discipleship
Swami Kriyananda

The Hindu Way of Awakening
Swami Kriyananda

Rays of the One Light
Swami Kriyananda

The Promise of Immortality
Swami Kriyananda

Religion in the New Age
Swami Kriyananda

Out of the Labyrinth
Swami Kriyananda

Art as a Hidden Message
Swami Kriyananda

Finding Happiness Day by Day
Swami Kriyananda

In Divine Friendship
Swami Kriyananda

Affirmations for Self-Healing
Swami Kriyananda

Cities of Light
Swami Kriyananda

Hope for a Better World
Swami Kriyananda

Your Sun Sign as a Spiritual Guide
Swami Kriyananda

Love Perfected, Life Divine
Swami Kriyananda

A Tale of Songs
Swami Kriyananda

Faith is my Armor
Devi Novak

AUM: The Melody of Love
Joseph Bharat Cornell

Spiritual Yoga
Gyandev McCord

Ask Asha
Asha Praver

From Bagels to Curry
Lila Devi

The JoyfulAthlete
George Beinhorn

Loved and Protected
Asha Praver

For Goodness' Sake
Michael Nitai Deranja

I Came from Joy
Lorna Ann Knox

Scary News
Lorna Ann Knox

**A Paramhansa Yogananda Trilogy
of Divine Love**
Sri Durga Mata

Divine Will Healing
Mary Kretzmann

**The Essential Flower Essesce
Handbook**
Lila Devi

Flower Essences for Animals
Lila Devi

The Healing Kitchen
Diksha McCord

Global Kitchen
Diksha McCord

Sharing Nature
Joseph Bharat Cornell

The Sky and Earth Touched Me
Joseph Bharat Cornell

Listening to Nature
Joseph Bharat Cornell

Chakras for Starters
Savitri Simpson

Soul Journey from Lincoln to Lindbergh
Richard Salva

Through Many Lives
Savitri Simpson

Through The Chakras
Savitri Simpson

Protectors Diary (Vol. 1): The Fifth Force
Joseph Selbie

Protectors Diary (Vol. 2): The Six
Joseph Selbie

The Flawless Mirror
Kamala Silva

The Light of the Christ Within
Reverend John Laurence, edited by Elana Joan Cara

Swami Kriyananda As We Have Known Him
Asha Praver